JANE AUSTEN

Emma

Retold by Margaret Tarner

Founding Editor: John Milne

The Macmillan Readers provide a choice of enjoyable reading materials for learners of English. The series is published at six levels – Starter, Beginner, Elementary, Pre-intermediate, Intermediate and Upper.

Level control

Information, structure and vocabulary are controlled to suit the students' ability at each level.

The number of words at each level:

Starter	about 300 basic words
Beginner	about 600 basic words
Elementary	about 1100 basic words
Pre-intermediate	about 1400 basic words
Intermediate	about 1600 basic words
Upper	about 2200 basic words

Vocabulary

Some difficult words and phrases in this book are important for understanding the story. Some of these words are explained in the story and some are shown in the pictures. From Pre-intermediate level upwards, words are marked with a number like this: ...[3]. These words are explained in the Glossary at the end of the book.

Answer keys

Answer keys for the *Points for Understanding* and the *Exercises* sections can be found at www.macmillanenglish.com

Contents

A Note About the Author and Life in the Nineteenth Century

Jane Austen was born on 16th December, 1775 at Steventon, Hampshire – a county[1] in the south of England. Jane's father was a clergyman[2] in the church at Steventon. Jane had six brothers – James, George, Edward, Henry and Charles – and one sister – Cassandra. Jane Austen's father made sure that his children had a good education. Jane learnt French, Italian and music. She studied English literature and poetry.

In 1803, Mr Austen and his family moved to Bath, a town in the west of England. Bath was popular and fashionable in the nineteenth century. People went there to meet friends and to drink the water from the warm springs that came out of the ground. They believed that the water was good for their health. In Bath, people played games of cards, and danced at balls in large buildings called The Assembly Rooms. They also listened to music and watched plays in the theatres. The visitors bought jewels and fashionable clothes in the shops. They walked in the wide streets and fine parks[3].

In 1805, Jane Austen's father died and the family moved to Southampton, in Hampshire. They lived there for only a few years. In 1810, the family moved again, to Chawton, in Hampshire. From that year, until her death in 1817, Jane was very busy. She wrote books, she visited her relatives[4], and she travelled round England with friends. Jane's brother, Edward, lived with Thomas and Catherine Knight. Mr and Mrs Knight had a large house – Godmersham Park – in the county of Kent. Jane and her sister often visited Edward at Godmersham Park. From her diaries and letters we can see that Jane was a very kind and intelligent woman.

Jane Austen never got married. Some people think that she fell in love in 1801, but the love affair did not end well.

The young man did not have any money and they could not marry. Her lover died suddenly, a few years later.

In 1802, Harris Bigg-Wither asked Jane Austen to marry him. However, Jane and Harris were engaged for only one day. The following morning, Jane changed her mind[5]. She decided not to marry Mr Bigg-Wither.

In 1811, Jane Austen's first book was published. Not many women writers were published at this time. Publishers did not like publishing books by women. For this reason, many women writers used men's names when they wrote books. However, Jane Austen never used a man's name. Her books were published using her own name and her stories were extremely popular. Her books were: *Sense and Sensibility* (1811), *Pride and Prejudice* (1813), *Mansfield Park* (1814), *Emma* (1815), *Northanger Abbey* (1818), *Persuasion* (1818) and *Sanditon* (unfinished).

Jane Austen's stories were not about poor people. She wrote about people who had money and property – houses and land. These very rich and powerful people were the 'polite society' of Britain. Few people from polite society worked to earn money. Men inherited[6] money and property from their fathers. The eldest son usually received most of the money and property after his father's death. If younger sons did not choose to join the army, or the navy, they became lawyers or clergymen.

People in polite society spent a lot of time calling on each other – visiting each others' houses. Each person who called at the house of a friend left a visiting card[7]. A servant then passed the card to the owner of the house. It was very impolite to call and not leave a visiting card, if the owner of the house was out.

People in polite society had dinner parties and dances in their homes. They played music and read books. They had conversations about art, music, poetry and politics. Men

5

went out onto their land to hunt with dogs and guns. Women read poetry and they painted pictures. They also walked in the gardens, or they rode horses in the grounds of their large properties. In winter, men and women from polite society often left their country houses and stayed in London for a few months.

Young women hoped to meet a suitable[8] young man and get married. It was important for a girl to marry a man who had money and property. If a girl did not have any money of her own and she did not marry, her life was very much more difficult.

Good manners – the correct way that people behaved and spoke – were very important. Well-educated people who had good manners spoke quietly and intelligently. They thought about other peoples' feelings and they made sure that they did not upset them.

Men and women in polite society talked about each other in a formal way. They used the titles *Lord*, *Sir*, *Mr*, *Mrs* or *Miss* in front of their last names. If they did not know the members of a family very well, people used *Miss* (+ their last name) when they spoke to elder, unmarried daughters. And they used *Miss* (+ their first name) when they spoke to younger, unmarried daughters. Married women would often be called by their husband's name. For example: Mrs John Knightley. Men often used only their last names when they spoke about each other. For example: Knightley or Elton.

Young women had to be introduced to young men whom they did not know. After that, they could talk to them.

In polite society, women did not travel alone or visit places alone. There were no cars, or trains, or bicycles at this time. People travelled in carriages pulled by horses, or they rode horses, or they walked.

NOTE: Knightley and Campbell are pronounced, **nightly** and **cambell**.

The Places in This Story

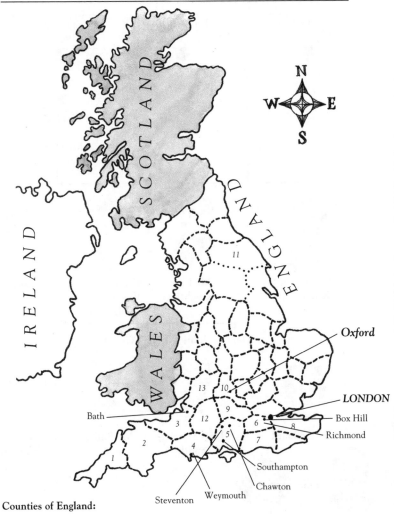

Counties of England:

1 CORNWALL 2 DEVON 3 SOMERSET 4 DORSET 5 HAMPSHIRE 6 SURREY
7 SUSSEX 8 KENT 9 BERKSHIRE 10 OXFORDSHIRE 11 YORKSHIRE 12 WILTSHIRE
13 GLOUCESTERSHIRE

7

The People in This Story

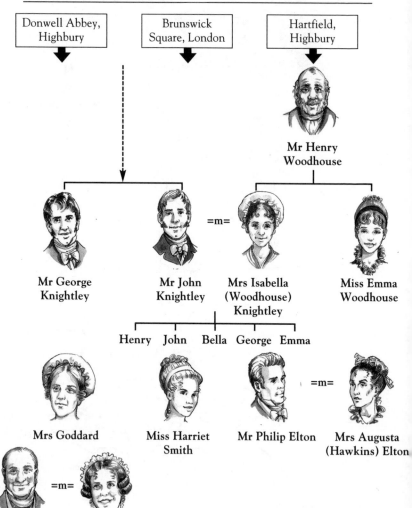

Donwell Abbey, Highbury	Brunswick Square, London	Hartfield, Highbury

Mr Henry Woodhouse

Mr George Knightley

Mr John Knightley =m= Mrs Isabella (Woodhouse) Knightley

Miss Emma Woodhouse

Henry   John   Bella   George   Emma

Mrs Goddard

Miss Harriet Smith

Mr Philip Elton =m= Mrs Augusta (Hawkins) Elton

Mr Cole =m= Mrs Cole

Dr Perry =m= Mrs Perry

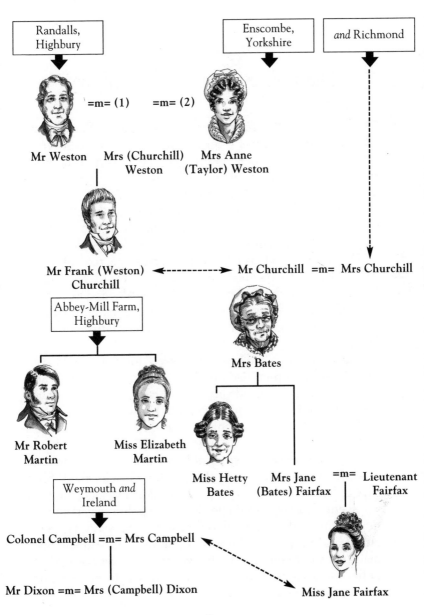

Randalls, Highbury

Enscombe, Yorkshire

and Richmond

=m= (1)   =m= (2)

Mr Weston   Mrs (Churchill) Weston   Mrs Anne (Taylor) Weston

Mr Frank (Weston) Churchill   ◄- - - - - - ►   Mr Churchill =m= Mrs Churchill

Abbey-Mill Farm, Highbury

Mrs Bates

Mr Robert Martin   Miss Elizabeth Martin

Weymouth and Ireland

Miss Hetty Bates   Mrs Jane (Bates) Fairfax   =m=   Lieutenant Fairfax

Colonel Campbell =m= Mrs Campbell

Mr Dixon =m= Mrs (Campbell) Dixon   Miss Jane Fairfax

9

1

The Polite Society of Highbury

The village of Highbury was in the county of Surrey and about sixteen miles from London. There were several large houses in the neighbourhood[9]. They were owned by the most important people in Highbury.

The largest house was called Donwell Abbey[10]. It was about a mile from the village and it was the home of Mr George Knightley who also owned much of the land in Highbury. Mr Knightley worked hard for the people of the neighbourhood and everybody liked and respected[11] him.

Mr Knightley's dearest friends were Miss Emma Woodhouse and her father, old Mr Henry Woodhouse. They lived in a large and comfortable house in Highbury, called Hartfield. Emma and her father were important people in Highbury.

Mr Woodhouse had been a widower[12] for many years. His wife, Emma's mother, had died when Emma was three years old. Mr Woodhouse lived very quietly. He did not often leave his home and call on other people. He worried about his health. He often thought that he was ill.

Emma Woodhouse, Mr Woodhouse's younger daughter, was nearly twenty-one years old. Because her mother was dead, Emma was in charge of everything at Hartfield. She gave orders to the servants and she decided how much money was spent. She was also the leader of the polite society in the neighbourhood. Emma Woodhouse was very pretty, very clever and very rich. She was charming[13] too and she had many friends. Emma always thought that she was right. Most of her friends agreed with her. Only Mr Knightley ever told her that she was wrong.

About five years earlier, Emma's elder sister, Isabella, had married Mr Knightley's younger brother, John. John Knightley was a clever lawyer who worked hard. He lived with his wife and five children in a large house in London. They all visited Hartfield when they could.

It was a cold evening in October. Emma Woodhouse and her father were sitting by the fire after dinner. They both looked sad.

That morning, Miss Anne Taylor, who had been Emma's governess[14] and friend for sixteen years, had left Hartfield to get married. Miss Taylor had married Mr Weston, a rich widower. Their home was Randalls, another large house, about half a mile from Hartfield.

Mr Woodhouse hated changes in his life and Miss Taylor's marriage had made him very unhappy. He sighed[15].

'I was very unhappy when your sister Isabella got married,' Mr Woodhouse said sadly. 'Why did Miss Taylor have to get married too? She was happy living with us here at Hartfield. Why has she left us?'

Emma smiled. 'Miss Taylor is now Mrs Weston, Papa[16],' she said. 'She married Mr Weston because she loves him. Mr Weston was born in the village. He is a good man. Mrs Weston will be happy at Randalls. It is a very comfortable house.'

'But Miss Taylor – er – Mrs Weston was happy *here*. Hartfield was her home,' Emma's father replied. 'Randalls may be a comfortable house, but Hartfield is a better place to live. It is much larger than Randalls. When shall I see Mrs Weston again? I cannot walk to Randalls. It is too far.'

'Then we shall take our carriage,' Emma told him. 'And the Westons can come here whenever they like.'

Mr Woodhouse sighed again, but he did not answer.

At that moment, Mr Knightley walked into the room.

11

He had been in London for a few days and the Woodhouses were delighted to see him.

Mr Knightley often visited Hartfield and he was always welcome there. He was a tall, handsome man and he was about thirty-seven years old. He had known Emma Woodhouse all her life.

'Did everything go well at the wedding of Miss Taylor and Mr Weston?' Mr Knightley asked cheerfully. 'I hope that it did not rain. Did anyone cry? Somebody always cries at a wedding!'

'It was a very sad occasion,' Mr Woodhouse replied. 'There was some rain this morning. I wanted Miss Taylor and Mr Weston to delay their wedding, but Mr Weston refused. He did not want to get married later. So now poor Miss Taylor has left Hartfield. I feel very sorry for her.'

'I can feel sorry for you and Emma, but not for Miss Taylor,' Mr Knightley said. 'She has only one person to please now, not two people.'

Emma laughed. 'And one of those two people is silly and thoughtless,' she said. 'That is what you are thinking, Mr Knightley.'

'You are right, my dear Emma,' her father said sadly. 'I am a silly and thoughtless old man.'

'Papa! I was talking about myself!' Emma said, laughing. 'Mr Knightley is always finding fault[17] with *me*, not finding fault with you.'

Emma looked at her friend and smiled.

'I do feel sad, Mr Knightley,' she said. 'But I am happy too. I made the match[18] between Miss Taylor and Mr Weston four years ago. I knew that they would marry one day. I planned everything.'

'Then please do not make any more matches, my dear Emma,' Mr Woodhouse told her. 'Whatever you plan comes true. You are always right.'

'I cannot stop matchmaking, Papa,' Emma said. 'Now I must help Mr Elton to find a wife. He has been the vicar of Highbury for a year. He lives in the vicarage alone. He must be lonely!'

'If you want to help Mr Elton, invite him to dinner,' Mr Woodhouse said. 'Young men always like good food and good company[19]. And ask Mr Knightley to dinner too. Then we shall have some good conversation.'

Mr Knightley laughed. 'That is a much better idea, sir,' he said. 'Invite Mr Elton to dinner, Emma. Give him some of your good food. But let him find his own wife. Mr Elton is twenty-six. He is old enough to find a wife for himself.'

But Emma had already chosen a wife for Mr Elton. Her name was Harriet Smith. She was seventeen years old and very pretty.

Harriet was a pupil at Mrs Goddard's school in Highbury. No one knew anything about the girl's family. But Emma was sure that Harriet's father was a gentleman[20].

Harriet Smith was short and plump[21]. She had beautiful blue eyes and fair hair. Harriet had good manners and a sweet smile, but she was not very clever. Harriet admired[22] Emma very much and she was delighted to be her friend.

Mr Knightley did not approve of Emma's friendship with Harriet Smith. He did not think that the two young women should be friends. He spoke to Mrs Weston about it when he visited her at Randalls a few days later.

'Harriet is not a good friend for Emma,' Mr Knightley said. 'She flatters[23] Emma too much.'

'But Emma can teach Harriet many things,' Mrs Weston replied. 'Emma has made plans to read with Harriet. She wants to improve Harriet's education. She has already made a list of suitable books.'

'Emma has been making lists and plans ever since she was a child,' Mr Knightley said quickly. 'She needs someone to make her think. Emma is intelligent. She has a good mind and she should use it.'

Mrs Weston smiled. 'Emma is also very beautiful,' she said, praising[24] her friend. 'Do you not think so, Mr Knightley?'

'Well, she is pretty and I like looking at her,' Mr Knightley replied.

'Emma is beautiful,' Mrs Weston said again. 'Her hazel[25] eyes are so bright and lively! Her complexion and figure[26] are perfect. She is a good daughter, sister and friend. But she does not like to be given advice. Please remember that.'

'I have been giving Emma advice for years,' Mr Knightley said smiling. 'But perhaps you are right. I shall say nothing about her friendship with Harriet Smith. I shall keep my thoughts to myself.'

Mr Knightley stood up to leave. 'I do think about what will happen to Emma,' he added. 'She says that she will never marry. But who knows what will happen to her in the future?'

Mrs Weston smiled. Emma and Mr Knightley were good friends, but nothing more. They were not in love with each other – they were fond of[27] each other. Mrs Weston was pleased. The Westons had other plans for Emma.

Many years before, Mr Weston had been a soldier. He had been a captain in the army. When he was a young man, he had fallen in love with Miss Churchill. Her family lived in Enscombe, in the county of Yorkshire. The Churchill family was very rich. When Captain Weston married Miss Churchill, her brother and his wife were very angry.

Three years later, Captain Weston's young wife was dead and he was a widower with a little boy named Frank. Captain Weston's brother-in-law and his wife felt very sorry for the little boy. The Churchills knew that Captain Weston could not look after his young son. They were very rich and they offered the little boy a fine home and a good education.

'Well, she is pretty and I like looking at her.'

Captain Weston agreed. Mr and Mrs Churchill became Frank's guardians[28] and they gave him their family name – Churchill.

Captain Weston became a merchant when he left the army. He made money in trade[29]. Twenty years later, he returned to Highbury. By this time, he was a rich man. He now called himself Mr Weston. He bought a fine large house called Randalls and lived there alone until his marriage with Miss Taylor.

Mr Weston sometimes went to London and saw his son Frank Churchill. The young man had never been to Highbury, but he promised to visit his father and his stepmother as soon as he could.

Mr and Mrs Weston thought that Frank would be a good match for Emma Woodhouse. They wanted the two young people to marry. That was the Westons' plan. But they kept these thoughts to themselves.

2

Harriet Smith

Harriet Smith lived at Mrs Goddard's school, but Emma often invited the pretty girl to Hartfield. Very soon, Harriet was given her own room in the Woodhouses' home. She saw Emma nearly every day and listened carefully to all her advice.

In the summer, Harriet had stayed with the Martins of Abbey-Mill Farm. The farm was on Mr Knightley's land, near Donwell Abbey. The farm was owned by Mr Knightley and Robert Martin looked after it for him.

Harriet talked a lot about the Martins. She told Emma about the size of the farm, the different animals and the kind Martin family.

Emma noticed this and she decided to find out more about them.

'Mr Knightley says that the Martins work very hard,' Emma said one day. 'Mrs Martin, her daughter and son-in-law look after the farm well.'

'Oh, Mr Martin – Mr Robert Martin – is Mrs Martin's son. He is not her son-in-law,' Harriet said, laughing. 'Mr Martin is not married. He looks after the farm because his father is dead. Mr Robert Martin is a very pleasant young man and he was very kind to me. And his sister, Elizabeth, was kind too.'

Emma smiled and thought, 'Is Harriet interested in Robert Martin? Does she hope to marry him?' This was not part of Emma's plan for her young friend.

'The Martins are good people, I am sure, but they are farmers,' Emma said. 'You are my friend now, Harriet. You are meeting the best people in Highbury. I am Emma Woodhouse of Hartfield. The Martins can never be my friends, so they cannot be your friends. You must stop visiting them at once.'

Harriet's blue eyes filled with tears.

'Oh, Miss Woodhouse ... I ... yes ... I am sure that you are right,' she said. 'You have been so kind to me. I love coming to Hartfield. I understand you, Miss Woodhouse.' Then she added sadly, 'I will not go to Abbey-Mill Farm again.'

Emma was pleased with Harriet's answer.

'Good. Harriet, you must learn to choose your friends more carefully now,' she said. 'You are meeting real gentlemen at Hartfield. Mr Knightley is the finest gentleman in Highbury. And Mr Elton, our vicar, is a gentleman too. He often comes to dinner at Hartfield.'

'Mr Elton is a very polite young man. He is handsome too,' Harriet said slowly.

'And you are a very pretty girl, 'Emma replied. 'Mr Elton can see that. He is very interested in you, Harriet.'

Harriet was pleased. Mr Elton, a gentleman, was interested in her! Miss Woodhouse said this, so it must be true.

Mr Elton came to Hartfield that evening. Emma began to speak to him about Harriet.

'Harriet Smith is a very pretty girl, is she not, Mr Elton?' Emma said to the young vicar. 'I have decided to paint a portrait of her. What do you think, Mr Elton?'

'I think that the portrait will be beautiful!' Mr Elton said quickly. 'You are such a good artist, Miss Woodhouse! Anything that you do is perfect! I should very much like to see your painting of Miss Smith!'

Emma had begun many portraits of her family, but she had never finished them. She was now excited about painting a portrait of Harriet.

She began the work the following day.

Mr Elton watched as Emma began to draw, and then to paint Harriet's portrait. He came to Hartfield every day until the portrait was finished.

'It is a very pretty painting, Emma, my dear,' said Mr Woodhouse. 'But in your portrait, Harriet is sitting in the garden. She is not wearing a shawl[30]! She will catch a cold[31]!'

Mr Knightley looked at the portrait too.

'You have made Harriet too tall, Emma,' he said.

'Oh, no, no!' Mr Elton cried. 'This portrait of Miss Smith is perfect! Miss Woodhouse is so very clever!'

Then Mr Elton added, 'A beautiful portrait must have a beautiful frame[32]. Let me take the painting to London for you, Miss Woodhouse. I shall get it framed there.'

Emma was very pleased. 'Mr Elton is in love with Harriet, I am sure,' she said to herself. 'My plan is going well. Soon Mr Elton will ask Harriet to marry him.'

———

'Let me take the painting to London for you, Miss Woodhouse.
I shall get it framed there.'

That evening, Harriet came to Hartfield for dinner. She was holding a letter in her hand and she was crying.

'Please read this letter, Miss Woodhouse,' Harriet said. 'I want your advice. Please tell me what to do.'

Emma read the letter quickly. It was from Mr Robert Martin and it was a proposal of marriage! Mr Martin was asking Harriet to marry him!

'What must I do, Miss Woodhouse?' Harriet asked again.

'You must answer the letter, of course,' Emma replied.

'Yes, but what must I say, Miss Woodhouse?' Harriet cried. 'It is a good letter. My answer must be well written too. Please help me.'

'Write the letter yourself, Harriet. Then I shall read it,' Emma said. 'Mr Martin will be unhappy, but your refusal must be very clear.'

'My refusal?' Harriet repeated slowly. 'I have to tell him that I cannot marry him, Miss Woodhouse?'

'Of course,' Emma said. 'You must refuse him. You cannot marry a farmer, Harriet. You are my friend and I am Emma Woodhouse of Hartfield. You know that I have an important position in Highbury. I could never invite the wife of Mr Martin to my home.'

Harriet did not say another word. She wrote a letter of refusal to Robert Martin. Emma read the letter and it was sent at once.

Harriet was very quiet all the evening. Emma tried to make her happy.

'There is another man who is interested in you, my dear Harriet,' Emma said. 'I am speaking about our vicar, Mr Elton. Mr Elton is a gentleman.'

'Mr Elton?' Harriet repeated in surprise.

'Yes. He is in London now. He is looking at your portrait and thinking about you. He is in love with you, I am sure of it. You will soon have another marriage proposal, Harriet.'

Harriet looked much happier. She forgot Robert Martin and she began to think about Mr Elton.

———

The next day, Mr Knightley called at Hartfield. Emma was surprised when he began talking about Harriet.

'You have been a good friend to Harriet Smith,' he said. 'And now I think that she will have some good news for you.'

Emma was very surprised. Had Mr Elton been talking to Mr Knightley about his love for Harriet?

'Robert Martin came to see me two evenings ago,' Mr Knightley went on. 'He told me that he loved your friend Harriet Smith. He was going to write to her and propose marriage. It will be a good match. I know that you will be pleased. I expect that Harriet will be coming here soon to tell you her good news.'

'Mr Martin has already sent the letter,' Emma said quietly. 'Harriet has refused him.'

Mr Knightley stood up. He looked very surprised. 'I know that Harriet is a silly girl,' he said, 'but she has refused Robert Martin! Are you sure, Emma?'

'Yes. I saw the letter myself,' Emma replied.

Mr Knightley was very angry now.

'You saw the letter?' he said. 'No, Emma, you *wrote* it or you told Harriet what to write!'

'Perhaps I did,' Emma replied. 'But I was right. Robert Martin is not Harriet's equal[33].'

'No, he is far, far better,' Mr Knightley said angrily. 'No one knows anything about Harriet Smith's family. She is pretty and good tempered, but that is all. She has only a simple education and no sense. She was happy to know the Martins before she met you. You have spoilt[34] Harriet Smith by making her your friend, Emma. You have made Robert Martin very unhappy. Harriet may soon be unhappy too.'

'Why? I have introduced Harriet to people from good society,' Emma replied. 'She is a very beautiful girl. There is a much more suitable young man in Highbury who will be happy to marry her.'

Mr Knightley was more angry than before.

'If you are talking about Elton, you are wrong,' he said. 'I know that young man better than you do. He may praise Harriet, but he will never marry her. She is poor. Elton will marry a rich woman, as soon as he finds one. You have made a bad mistake, Emma. You have made a very bad mistake. Good afternoon.'

Emma smiled as Mr Knightley left the room. But his words had upset her. Emma did not want to quarrel[35] with Mr Knightley, but she knew that he was wrong.

Mr Elton brought back Harriet's portrait from London that afternoon. The painting had been beautifully framed. The portrait was soon hanging on a wall in the sitting-room at Hartfield. Every time that Mr Elton looked at the picture of the beautiful girl, he smiled.

Emma made sure that Harriet was always at Hartfield when Mr Elton came to dinner. Mr Elton was always smiling now. Emma thought that she knew why.

———

It was the middle of December, but the weather was fine. One morning, Emma and Harriet walked to a cottage which belonged to a poor family. They were taking food to them.

The road to the little cottage went past the vicarage. Harriet said that she wanted to see the inside of Mr Elton's house. Emma laughed.

'You will soon be married to Mr Elton and living there yourself,' she told Harriet. 'Then I shall be happy to visit you in your own home.'

Harriet blushed – her face became red – but she looked very happy.

'I am very surprised that you have not married, Miss Woodhouse,' Harriet said cheerfully. 'You are so beautiful and so clever ...'

'I am happy as I am,' Emma replied. 'I do not think that I shall ever marry. Why should I? I have my own home and a loving father. I have money too.'

'But if you do not marry, you will be like Miss Bates in the village,' Harriet said sadly. 'People will feel sorry for you.'

'Miss Bates is poor. That is why people feel sorry for her,' Emma replied. 'I am rich. I shall be busy and happy all my life. My sister has five children – my nephews and nieces. When I am old, I shall be able to enjoy their company.'

'Miss Bates has a niece,' Harriet said. 'Do you know her?'

'Oh, yes – Jane Fairfax,' Emma replied. 'Miss Bates is always talking about her. I am tired of hearing her name. I always have to meet Jane Fairfax when she comes to Highbury. Her aunt thinks that we are friends. But Jane is very cold and unfriendly. I do not like her.'

By now, Emma and Harriet had reached the poor family's little cottage. Emma spoke kindly to them and gave them the food.

Very soon, the two friends were on their way home again. After a few minutes, they saw Mr Elton walking towards them. The young vicar smiled.

'Good morning, Miss Woodhouse and Miss Smith,' Mr Elton said bowing[36] politely. 'Let me walk back to Hartfield with you.'

'If Harriet was alone, Mr Elton might propose to her,' Emma said to herself. Then she had an idea. As they came near to the vicarage, she began to walk more slowly.

'My bootlace[37] is loose. I must tie it,' Emma said. 'Please go on.'

Mr Elton and Harriet walked on together. Emma bent down quickly and broke the lace.

'Oh, dear!' Emma called out. 'My lace has broken! Mr Elton, may I go into your house? May I speak to your housekeeper[38]? Perhaps she can give me another lace.'

Mr Elton was delighted to help Miss Woodhouse. Soon they were all inside the vicarage. Emma went to see the housekeeper and left Mr Elton and Harriet together.

Emma talked to the housekeeper for as long as possible. Then she went to the sitting-room. When she entered the room, Mr Elton and Harriet were standing by the window. But after listening to their conversation for a few minutes, Emma was disappointed. Mr Elton was talking about food, not love.

'That young man is taking a long time to decide about marriage,' Emma thought to herself. 'But he will ask Harriet to marry him soon, I am sure of it.'

3

Mr Woodhouse Goes Out to Dinner

Another week passed and Mr Elton still had not proposed to Harriet. John Knightley was bringing his family to Highbury for the Christmas holiday and Emma was very busy getting Hartfield ready for their visit.

Mr Woodhouse was a kind man and he loved his family very much. But he was easily upset and he worried about many things. He worried most about his health and the health of his family. He did not like bad weather and any kind of travel. He hated change of every kind.

The weather was now very cold and the ground was hard and slippery with ice. Mr Woodhouse was very worried about the Knightleys' journey from London to Highbury.

'Sixteen miles is a long way,' he said. 'And the roads are bad at this time of year.'

However, the Knightleys all arrived safely and Mr Woodhouse was delighted to see his daughter Isabella and her children again.

Isabella – Mrs John Knightley – was very like her father. She worried about her health and her children's health. Isabella was not as clever as her younger sister, Emma, but she was very kind.

John Knightley, Emma's brother-in-law, was a clever and very successful lawyer. But he was not as pleasant as his brother George Knightley of Donwell Abbey. John Knightley became angry easily and he always said what he thought. Isabella was never upset by her husband's behaviour. She took no notice of it[39]. John Knightley liked to tease[40] his friends and relations and his words sometimes upset them or made them angry.

That evening, John's elder brother, Mr George Knightley, walked to Hartfield from his house, Donwell Abbey. He was dining with the Woodhouses too.

Mr Knightley and Emma had not spoken to each other since their quarrel.

Emma was holding her little niece in her arms when Mr Knightley came into the sitting-room. Emma looked up and saw that he was smiling at them both.

'Is not little Emma a beautiful child?' Emma said quietly, looking down at the baby.

'She is nearly as beautiful as her aunt,' Mr Knightley replied. 'We can agree on that if not on other things. Let us be friends again, my dearest Emma. Let us forget our quarrel.'

'I shall be pleased to forget it,' Emma said. 'I know that I am spoilt. I do not think that I was wrong about Harriet and Robert Martin. But I upset you and I am sorry. Shake hands with me, Mr Knightley. We have different ideas, but we can still be friends.'

They shook hands and the rest of the evening passed very pleasantly. Only Mr Woodhouse was unhappy.

'My dear Isabella, you look tired,' he said to his elder daughter. 'You and the children have had a tiring journey. You must all go to bed early tonight. Doctor Perry is coming to see me tomorrow. He will check that I am well. He can check the children too. We must look after their health while they are at Hartfield.'

'The children are all quite well, Papa,' Isabella said with a kind smile. 'And I am not tired at all.'

Soon Isabella began to talk about her good friends, Mrs and Miss Bates. She was pleased to hear that they were both well.

'And what about Miss Bates's niece, Jane Fairfax?' Isabella went on. 'Sometimes I see her in London, with her guardians, the Campbells. Jane is so clever and so beautiful, do you not agree, Emma? You could be such good friends if Jane lived in Highbury!'

'Emma has a friend – Miss Harriet Smith. She is a very pretty girl,' Mr Woodhouse said. 'Harriet often stays with us. You will see her here very soon.'

———

Time passed quickly and happily at Hartfield. Emma, Mr Woodhouse, Mr Knightley, and Isabella and John Knightley were invited to dine[41] with the Westons at Randalls on 24th December – Christmas Eve. Mr Elton and Harriet were also invited to the dinner party that evening.

Harriet had been staying at Hartfield, but then she caught a very bad cold. Isabella was afraid that her children would become ill too. So Harriet went back to the school where Mrs Goddard could look after her.

Emma went to see Harriet on the morning of 24th

December. The poor girl had a sore throat and her face was very pale.

'You cannot come to Randalls tonight. You are too ill,' Emma said. 'Mr Elton will be sorry that you are not there.'

As Emma left the school, she met Mr Elton himself and told him about Harriet's cold and sore throat.

'I am afraid that Harriet will have to stay at home tonight. She has a bad cold,' Emma said.

'And you have been visiting her, Miss Woodhouse!' Mr Elton said in surprise. 'That is not right. You must think of your own health.'

'*You* look rather pale, Mr Elton,' Emma told him. 'Perhaps *you* should stay at home too.'

Emma expected Mr Elton to agree. 'He could stay at home instead of going to dinner at Randalls,' she thought. 'He could think of Harriet. He could write her a loving letter ...'

But at that moment, they met John Knightley. He offered to take Mr Elton in his carriage to Randalls that evening and with a happy smile, Mr Elton agreed.

As Mr Elton walked away quickly, Emma's brother-in-law laughed.

'That young man always smiles when he sees you, Emma,' John Knightley said. 'I think that he is in love with you. Please be careful!' And he laughed again. He enjoyed teasing his sister-in-law.

'No, you are wrong. Mr Elton loves Miss Smith, not me,' Emma said. 'Mr Elton and I are good friends, nothing more.'

But John Knightley laughed once again and shook his head.

By the evening, the weather was extremely cold. Mr Woodhouse, Emma, Isabella and her husband were going to travel from Hartfield to Randalls in two carriages.

Mr Woodhouse went in his own carriage with Isabella. Emma went with John Knightley in his carriage and they drove to the vicarage to collect Mr Elton. The vicar was waiting for them with a happy smile. He smiled at Emma all the way to Randalls and did not stop praising her. John Knightley listened, but he said nothing.

Emma was worried. Did Mr Elton think that she loved him? No! It was impossible.

At dinner, Emma sat next to Mr Weston. He was talking about his son, Frank Churchill.

'Yes, we had a letter from Frank this morning,' Mr Weston said, smiling happily. 'My son is planning to visit us here in Highbury. He will be here in two weeks. His aunt, Mrs Churchill, is often ill and she does not like Frank to leave her. But he will come this time, I know.'

Emma was delighted to hear this news. She had always wanted to meet Mr Frank Churchill and she knew that Mrs Weston did too.

After dinner, Emma spoke to Mrs Weston about Frank's visit. 'I am looking forward to seeing Mr Frank Churchill at Highbury,' she said.

'I hope that Mrs Churchill will let him come,' Mrs Weston replied. 'She is a bad-tempered woman and she is very jealous of Mr Weston. She wants to keep Frank with her at Enscombe, if she can.'

'If Frank Churchill wants to come here, I am sure that he will,' Emma said.

The gentlemen came into the room where the ladies were sitting and everyone had tea. Mr Elton sat next to Emma. He was smiling more and more. He began talking about Harriet's sore throat. But Emma soon understood that he was worried about *her*, not Harriet.

'Miss Woodhouse must think about her own health, Mrs Weston,' the young vicar said. 'Miss Woodhouse is important to us all. Please tell her to be careful, Mrs Weston. She will listen to you.'

Mrs Weston was surprised at Mr Elton's words, but she said nothing. At that moment, John Knightley left the room for a few minutes. When he came back, he was smiling.

'Well, sir,' he said to Mr Woodhouse. 'We shall all have an exciting journey home. Snow has been falling for some time.'

Mr Woodhouse hated excitement and he especially hated bad weather. He looked worried and Isabella did too.

'My poor children!' she cried. 'I must get back to them tonight! Will the carriages be able to travel through the snow on the road?'

Everyone stood up and began talking at once. Mr Knightley looked at his brother John and frowned[42]. Then he left the room. He came back a few minutes later.

'There is very little snow,' Mr Knightley said quietly to Emma. 'John was teasing us. If you all leave now, you will have a safe journey home. Shall I tell the servants to bring the carriages to the door?'

'Yes, please do. Thank you,' Emma said quickly.

Soon everyone was ready to go. Mr Woodhouse slowly got into his own carriage and Isabella followed him. John Knightley got in too and the carriage moved on.

Emma got into the second carriage and she was followed by Mr Elton, who sat beside her. They were alone. Then Emma saw that Mr Elton had been drinking too much of Mr Weston's good wine.

As the carriage began to move, Mr Elton took Emma's hand and held it in his own.

'My dear Miss Woodhouse!' he cried. 'I cannot hide my feelings any longer! They are too strong. You must know how much I love you! Please accept my proposal of marriage and make me the happiest of men!'

Emma was angry, but she did not show her true feelings.

'Mr Elton, you should be saying these things to Harriet, not to me,' she said quietly.

'I cannot hide my feelings any longer. Please accept my proposal of marriage!'

'Miss Smith? I do not care for Miss Harriet Smith!' Mr Elton cried. 'I love you, Miss Woodhouse, only you.'

Emma was silent. She did not know what to say.

'You are making me very happy, Miss Woodhouse,' Mr Elton said, smiling. 'Your silence tells me that your feelings are the same as mine.'

'Mr Elton, you are *very* wrong,' Emma said angrily. 'I have no wish to marry anyone. And I would certainly never marry you.'

They sat silently until they reached the vicarage. Mr Elton got out of the carriage without saying another word and Emma was taken home to Hartfield. She did not sleep well that night. She had been very wrong about Mr Elton! He had never loved Harriet Smith.

'That silly young man thinks that he is my equal!' Emma thought. 'I cannot believe it. Mr Knightley and his brother John were right about Mr Elton and I was wrong.'

Then Emma thought again about Harriet. Her friend would soon have to be told the truth. Mr Elton had never loved the poor girl. But Emma was still sure of one thing. She was glad that Harriet had refused to marry Mr Martin. The pretty girl could make a better match than the young farmer.

4

Frank Churchill

On Christmas Day, the ground was covered with snow. The Woodhouses and John Knightley and his family did not go out to pray in the church. The only visitor at Hartfield was Mr Knightley.

Emma felt more cheerful. She had decided not to tell anyone about Mr Elton's proposal of marriage. The weather was too bad for Harriet to visit Hartfield and Emma was pleased.

A few days later, the weather had improved. It was not so cold and most of the snow had disappeared. John Knightley and his family got ready to leave Hartfield and return to their home in London. Mr Woodhouse wanted Isabella to stay longer, but she had decided to go home. She was never happy when she was apart from her husband and children.

That same evening, Mr Woodhouse received a very polite letter from Mr Elton. The young man was leaving Highbury for a few weeks. He was going to stay with friends in Bath. Mr Elton sent Mr Woodhouse his good wishes, but said nothing about Emma.

All that night, Mr Woodhouse worried about Mr Elton's journey to Bath.

Emma told Harriet the truth about Mr Elton's feelings the next day. Harriet was very upset. The pretty girl cried and cried, but she did not blame[43] Emma. Harriet blamed herself. Mr Elton was a gentleman. He could never love her. She knew that now.

Emma invited Harriet to stay at Hartfield. She tried to help her friend to forget Mr Elton.

The Westons had been expecting Frank Churchill to visit them at Randalls, but he did not come. Mrs Churchill was ill again and Frank could not leave her.

'Mrs Weston is very disappointed,' Emma said to Mr Knightley. 'I am sorry too, but Mr Weston now hopes that his son will come in the spring.'

'I cannot understand that young man,' Mr Knightley said angrily. The name of Frank Churchill always made Mr Knightley angry.

'He must be very selfish,' Mr Knightley went on. 'I know

that Mrs Churchill is a difficult woman. But Frank Churchill could come to Highbury if he wanted to. He has plenty of money and plenty of time. I heard that the young man was on holiday in Weymouth in the summer. So he *can* leave Enscombe when he wants to.

'Frank Churchill must do his duty[44],' Mr Knightley went on. 'And that duty is to visit his father and his stepmother, Mrs Weston. He should tell Mrs Churchill this.'

Emma laughed. 'Mr Knightley, you do not understand,' she said. 'Frank Churchill is dependent[45] on the Churchills. They have given him money and a good education. It is his duty to please *them*.'

'It is his duty now to please his father,' Mr Knightley replied. 'Frank Churchill has enough time to go on holiday by the sea. He has enough time to write long letters to the Westons. He must find enough time to visit Highbury too.'

'You want to think badly of Frank Churchill,' Emma said. 'You have never met him, but you do not like him.'

'That is not true,' Mr Knightley replied. 'I do not want to think badly of him. I am sure that Frank Churchill is a fine young man, with very good manners.'

'Then he will be welcome in Highbury,' Emma told her friend. 'How excited everyone will be when he comes at last!'

'I do not care if he comes or not,' Mr Knightley said. 'I am not a silly young girl. I have no interest in Mr Frank Churchill. I refuse to talk about him any more!'

———

A few days later, Emma and Harriet were walking together in Highbury. Harriet still wanted to talk about Mr Elton and everything in Highbury reminded her of him.

Soon they were passing the house where Mrs Bates and her daughter, Miss Hetty Bates, lived.

The two ladies lived in a very small house in the centre of

the village. The Bateses had very little money, so they had very few pleasures. They could not buy good wine, fine food or expensive clothes. They were delighted when visitors called on them and they were both very fond of Emma.

Emma knew that it was her duty to visit the Bateses more often. But she thought that the ladies were very dull[46]. Old Mrs Bates was very deaf[47]. Miss Bates was always talking about her niece, Jane Fairfax, and reading Jane's latest letter to her visitors.

On that morning, Emma was tired of hearing Harriet talk about Mr Elton. So she said to her young friend, 'Perhaps we should call on Mrs and Miss Bates. Their lives are very dull. It is our duty to make them happier.'

Miss Bates began talking as soon as her visitors came into the sitting-room.

'My dear Miss Woodhouse! My dear Miss Smith! What a pleasure it is to see you in our little house!' she cried. 'How is dear Mr Woodhouse? Our dear friend, Mrs Cole, has just left. She was talking about Mr Elton. It is a pity[48] that he has gone to Bath. How we shall all miss him! He has such good manners — and such a pleasant smile!

'Mrs Cole was kind enough to eat some of my cake,' Miss Bates went on. 'Do sit down, Miss Woodhouse. Perhaps you and Miss Smith will have some cake too?'

Emma smiled politely and accepted a piece of cake. Miss Bates soon began talking about her niece, Jane Fairfax.

'Yes, our dear Jane is in Bath too. Everyone there admires her. She dances so beautifully, of course, and she is so clever.'

'Have you had a letter from Miss Fairfax recently?' Emma asked politely. 'I hope that she is well.'

'Thank you, Miss Woodhouse, thank you. Yes, we had a letter from Jane this morning! It is so kind of you to ask about her! Now, where is it? Yes, here it is! It is just a short letter, this time — only two pages.'

'Yes, we had a letter from Jane this morning!'

'Miss Fairfax has beautiful handwriting,' Emma said.

'Oh, thank you,' replied Miss Bates quickly. 'Mother, did you hear that? Miss Woodhouse has given us her opinion[49] about Jane's handwriting. She says that Jane has beautiful handwriting — BEAUTIFUL HANDWRITING!' she said again, more loudly.

'My mother is rather deaf,' Miss Bates said with a smile. 'I sometimes have to say things more than once. But Mother can always hear what Jane says. Dear Jane speaks so very clearly. It will be delightful to see her again!'

'Is Miss Fairfax coming here soon?' Emma asked. She was surprised. 'She has not been in Highbury for more than two years, I think.'

'You are right, Miss Woodhouse,' Miss Bates said happily. 'You have remembered the time exactly. Yes, Jane will be here next week!'

'Next week!' Emma repeated in surprise.

'Yes, next week,' Miss Bates said with a smile. 'It is all in her letter. And she will be staying with us for three months. Mother and I are so pleased.'

'How can Miss Fairfax be away from the Campbells for so long?' Emma asked.

'Oh, the Campbells, dear Jane's guardians, are going to Ireland,' Miss Bates replied. 'Their own daughter — such a plain girl — has married a Mr Dixon. Mr and Mrs Dixon have a house in Ireland. The Dixons are very fond of Jane. They all visited Weymouth together — Mr Dixon saved Jane before she fell into the sea!'

Emma was interested and her clever mind was busy at once. 'Why is Jane not going to Ireland?' she thought. 'Perhaps Mr Dixon, whose wife is very plain, is too fond of the beautiful Jane Fairfax.'

Emma wanted to know more.

'I am surprised that Miss Fairfax is not going to Ireland,'

she said. 'Mrs Dixon is Miss Fairfax's dear friend, I believe.'

'That is true — very true,' Miss Bates replied. 'Mr and Mrs Dixon both wanted Jane to go with them. But our dear niece has been ill. Jane caught a cold in November and has not been well since then. If she comes to Highbury, Mother and I can look after her. Jane is always happy here — as you know, Miss Woodhouse.

'But you must read dear Jane's letter for yourself,' said Miss Bates, picking up some pages from a chair. 'She explains everything so clearly!'

Emma stood up quickly. 'I am afraid that we must go now,' she said. 'My father is waiting for us. Thank you so much for telling us about Miss Fairfax.'

As they walked back to Hartfield, Harriet asked Emma to tell her all about Jane.

'Why does Jane Fairfax live with the Campbells and not here in Highbury with Mrs and Miss Bates?' Harriet said.

'It is an interesting story,' Emma replied. 'Jane Bates, Mrs Bates's younger daughter, married a soldier named Lieutenant Fairfax. He was killed, fighting for his country, soon after baby Jane was born. Before he died, Lieutenant Fairfax saved the life of Colonel Campbell. Then, when Jane Fairfax was three years old, her mother died and Jane became an orphan.

'The Campbells looked after Jane as well as their own daughter,' Emma continued. 'And when Jane was nine years old, they became her guardians. The Campbells gave Jane a good home and a good education and she has lived with them ever since.'

'So the Campbells are rich,' Harriet said.

'No, they are not,' Emma replied. 'If Jane does not marry, she may have to become a governess. She has had a good education and she is clever. She will do well.

'Let us talk about someone else, Harriet!' Emma said. 'I am tired of Jane Fairfax! I was hoping that Frank Churchill was coming to Highbury, not Jane. I am far more interested in Frank.'

Emma did not like Jane Fairfax, but she did not know why. The two girls were the same age and they should have been friends.

5

Jane Fairfax

It was now February. Emma soon gave Mr Knightley the news that Jane was coming to Highbury.

'I am pleased to hear it,' Mr Knightley said. 'She will be a better friend for you than Harriet Smith. You do not like Jane because she is better educated than you, Emma. She reads many more books and she plays the piano better than you do. She is a very beautiful and a very clever young woman.'

'Yes, but she is so cold,' Emma had replied. 'I do not enjoy her company. It is difficult to talk to Jane Fairfax. I never know what she is thinking. Her aunt talks too much and Jane Fairfax does not talk enough!'

But when Jane arrived in Highbury, Emma felt that she had been very unkind to her.

Jane was tall and she had a good figure. She had beautiful dark grey eyes and dark brown hair. Her skin was pale and she had a lovely complexion. Everyone agreed that Miss Fairfax was very charming.

Emma decided to be more friendly towards the beautiful girl and she soon invited Jane, Mrs Bates and Miss Bates to spend the evening at Hartfield.

But after one evening, Emma's unkind feelings about Jane

Fairfax returned. Emma decided that she did not want to see Jane again. She had asked Jane many questions about the Dixons. But Jane's answers were very short and they did not give Emma much information.

Then Emma found out that Jane had met Frank Churchill in Weymouth.

'You have met Mr Frank Churchill, Miss Fairfax? You are so lucky!' Emma cried. 'Everyone in Highbury wants to see Mr Frank Churchill! Is he handsome?'

'People think that he is,' Jane replied.

'And does he talk well? What about his manners and his conversation?'

'People say that his manners are good,' Jane said quietly. But she refused to give an opinion of her own.

The next morning Mr Knightley came to speak to Mr Woodhouse about business. Mr Knightley had also been at Hartfield the previous evening. He began to talk with Emma about her guests.

'I had a very pleasant time last night,' Mr Knightley said. 'You and Jane gave us some good music, Emma. And you gave us some good conversation.'

Emma smiled. 'Jane certainly plays the piano very well,' she said. 'But her conversation is not interesting. Jane said very little all the evening. She did not answer any of my questions. She is not good company.'

Mr Knightley looked unhappy. 'I would like you to be friends with Jane,' he said.

'Jane does not make friends easily,' Emma replied. 'But she is very beautiful and very charming. I admire her, but I feel sorry for her too. Her life will not be easy, like mine.'

Mr Knightley was pleased at Emma's words but Mr Woodhouse looked sad.

'The Bateses do not have an easy life either,' he said. 'They have very little money. I wish that we could do more for them, Emma, my dear. Ah! We have just killed one of our pigs here at Hartfield. Perhaps we could send Miss Bates some of the meat?'

'Papa, do not worry,' Emma said. 'I have already sent a large piece of the pork to Miss and Mrs Bates's house.'

Mr Knightley was about to speak when the sitting-room door opened and Miss Bates and Miss Fairfax came in.

'Oh, Miss Woodhouse!' Miss Bates cried. 'We have come to thank you for the piece of pork! You are so very kind! And we have some news to tell you. You will never believe it but — Mr Elton is to be married! Yes, married! He is getting married to Miss Augusta Hawkins of Bath. We shall all have a new neighbour at Highbury. What do you think about that, Miss Woodhouse?'

'I am sure that everyone will wish Mr Elton happiness,' Emma said quietly. 'And Miss Hawkins too, of course.'

Emma turned towards Jane Fairfax. 'What do you think about the news, Miss Fairfax?'

'I do not know Mr Elton, so I can have no opinion,' Jane replied.

'And Mr Elton has only been away four weeks,' Miss Bates said. 'I did think at one time — perhaps a young lady in Highbury — but no! Mr Elton is a fine young man ...

'Well, Jane,' Miss Bates went on, 'we must be going now. Your grandmamma will be waiting for us. She will be worried. I think that it is going to rain! Oh, Mr Knightley, are you leaving too? Goodbye, Mr Woodhouse and dear Miss Woodhouse. Mr Elton — marrying Miss Hawkins! She will be Mrs Elton — a new neighbour! It is so exciting!'

A few minutes after this, the rain began to fall heavily. As soon as the rain had stopped, Emma had another visitor.

'Oh, Miss Woodhouse, what do you think has happened!' Harriet cried as she ran into the room.

Emma thought that her friend had heard about Mr Elton.

But that news would have made Harriet upset. Harriet looked very happy.

'I was in Mrs Ford's shop in Highbury, when they came in,' Harriet went on. 'I did not know what to do.'

'What do you mean? Who came in?' Emma asked her friend.

'Why, Elizabeth Martin and her brother, of course,' Harriet replied. 'I did not know what to do. I could not leave the shop, because it was raining hard. Then Elizabeth came to talk to me and she was so kind. Mr Robert Martin spoke to me too. Oh, Miss Woodhouse, I was so happy when he spoke to me. Now I do not know what to think. Please help me!'

At first, Emma had no answer.

'The Martins behaved well,' she said after a few minutes. 'And you did too, Harriet. It was very difficult for you. But it is over now. You must stop thinking about that meeting. You will never see the Martins here at Hartfield. It may be months before you see them again.'

'Yes, of course, dear Miss Woodhouse,' Harriet said sadly.

'And now I have news for you,' Emma said.

The news about Mr Elton's engagement was a shock for Harriet. She stopped talking about the Martins at once. All her conversation was now about Miss Hawkins of Bath. Mr Elton loved Miss Hawkins, so she must be very beautiful!

———

Two days later, the Westons saw Emma walking by herself in Highbury. They stopped their carriage and began to talk to her.

'We were coming to Hartfield to tell you the news,' Mrs Weston said. 'Frank Churchill will be here tomorrow.'

'Yes, Frank is coming at last,' said Mr Weston. 'Here is his letter. He will be here tomorrow at about three o'clock. He is staying for two weeks.'

'I shall be so happy to have Frank with us at Randalls,'

Mrs Weston said. 'We shall bring him to Hartfield very soon, Emma.'

But Frank Churchill surprised everyone. He arrived a day early. By twelve o'clock the following morning, Mr Weston and Frank Churchill were talking with Mr Woodhouse in the sitting-room at Hartfield.

As soon as Emma came into the sitting-room, Mr Weston introduced Frank to her. Emma saw a tall and very handsome young man who had very good manners.

Frank Churchill was also a very good talker. He had ideas and opinions about everything. Emma was soon enjoying his company very much.

'I believe that I know a neighbour of yours, Miss Woodhouse,' Frank Churchill said. 'The lady's name is Fairfax, but the family's name is Barnes or Bates, I think. Do you know them?'

'We all know the Bateses. They are our good friends,' Mr Weston said. 'You met Jane Fairfax in Weymouth, I think, Frank. You must visit Miss and Mrs Bates. They will be glad to see you.'

'There is no hurry,' Frank said. 'Any day will do. Yes, I did meet Miss Fairfax in Weymouth. She was there with the Campbells.'

'Please visit the Bateses today, Frank,' his father said. 'Old Mrs Bates is Jane's grandmother. Mrs Bates and her daughter Hetty are very poor. It would be very impolite if you do not visit Jane.'

As Mr Weston and his son were leaving, Emma spoke to Frank. 'Jane Fairfax is a very elegant young lady,' she said.

'Yes, I suppose so,' said Frank quietly.

Emma was surprised. She had thought that a young man like Mr Frank Churchill would be interested in the elegant and charming Miss Fairfax.

Frank Churchill visited Hartfield again the next day. This

time, he came with Mrs Weston. The young man seemed to like his stepmother very much. Emma was delighted.

The weather that day was good. Frank, Emma and Mrs Weston walked in the garden at Hartfield and then they went into the village of Highbury itself.

Frank Churchill wanted to see everything and everything in Highbury pleased him. They all stopped outside the Crown Inn. When Frank heard that the inn had a ballroom, he became very excited. He wanted to see inside the room at once.

'This room is perfect for dancing!' Frank Churchill said, as he looked around. 'We must have a ball while I am in Highbury! I am sure that there are plenty of young people here who would enjoy dancing at a ball!'

After several minutes Frank, Emma and Mrs Weston left the inn and walked on. They were soon outside the house where Mrs and Miss Bates lived.

'Did you visit the Bateses yesterday?' Emma asked Frank Churchill.

'Yes, I did,' Frank replied. 'I saw all three ladies – Mrs and Miss Bates and Miss Fairfax. Miss Bates did not stop talking for more than half an hour!'

'Did you think that Miss Fairfax was looking well?' Emma asked.

'No, I did not think that she looked well. Not well at all,' Frank said quickly. 'She is always pale, but now she looks ill.'

'Did you often see Miss Fairfax in Weymouth?' Emma asked.

'Yes, I met her and the Campbells quite often,' Frank replied. 'And I met Mr Dixon too, of course. He was not married to Miss Campbell then. Mr Dixon admired Miss Fairfax. And he admired how she played the piano too. Have you heard Miss Fairfax play the piano, Miss Woodhouse?'

They all stopped outside the Crown Inn.

'Yes, I have,' Emma replied. 'And I agree with Mr Dixon. Miss Fairfax plays very well.'

'Miss Fairfax does everything extremely well,' Frank said, smiling. 'However, Mr Dixon married Miss Campbell. I do not know what Miss Fairfax thought about that. You have been Miss Fairfax's friend longer than I have.'

'I cannot say that I am Miss Fairfax's friend,' Emma said. 'She is very reserved[50] and it is difficult to know her. I often think that she is hiding something – that she has a secret.'

'I agree with you,' Frank Churchill said. 'It is difficult to be fond of a reserved person.'

Emma was very pleased with Mr Frank Churchill. His conversation was interesting and amusing. He was charming and he had good manners. Emma enjoyed his company. But she was very surprised when Frank went away the next day. He rode to London, to have his hair cut. Mr Weston laughed, but Mrs Weston shook her head.

Mr Knightley had not approved of Frank Churchill from the first time that he had heard about him. When Emma told Mr Knightley about Frank's visit to London, he was silent for a moment. Then he said, 'It is just as I thought. Frank Churchill is a silly, spoilt young man.'

6

An Invitation From the Coles

The Coles had lived in Highbury for several years. Because Mr Cole was a merchant and had made money in trade, Miss Woodhouse did not invite the Coles to Hartfield.

However, the Coles had now decided to give a dinner

party and they invited all the polite society of Highbury. Everyone received an invitation except Mr Woodhouse and Emma.

Emma had decided to refuse any invitation from the Coles. But she was angry when she was not invited. Then at last, the invitation arrived. Inside it there was a handwritten note from Mrs Cole. She explained why the Woodhouses' invitation had arrived late. They had been waiting for a screen[51] to arrive from London. Mr Cole had bought the screen so that Mr Woodhouse would not feel any draughts in their house.

It was a kind thought and Emma changed her mind. She decided to accept the invitation from the Coles. But Mr Woodhouse could not accept the invitation. He did not like staying out late in the evenings. And meeting large groups of people upset him.

'Emma and I are not fond of big dinner parties,' Mr Woodhouse said to the Westons. 'I shall stay at home. But you and Mr Knightley can take care of Emma, so she should go.'

'I have asked Mrs Goddard and Mrs Bates to come to Hartfield on that evening, Papa,' Emma told her father. 'You can all have dinner together and then play cards. You will enjoy that.'

On the evening of the dinner party, the two old ladies arrived at Hartfield before Emma left. The three old friends all admired Emma's new dress very much.

Emma's carriage arrived at the Coles' house at the same time as Mr Knightley drove up in his own carriage.

'I am very glad that you came in your carriage and that you did not walk here, Mr Knightley,' Emma said. 'Everyone knows that you are a gentleman. Now you look like one. I shall be happy to go in with you.'

'Silly girl,' Mr Knightley said with a smile, as he and

Emma went into the house together.

Soon afterwards, the Westons arrived with Frank Churchill. The handsome young man looked round for Emma and hurried across the room to sit next to her. Frank Churchill and Emma Woodhouse sat next to each other at dinner too and they had long and interesting conversations.

It was a large dinner party, but Miss Bates, Miss Fairfax and Miss Smith had not been invited to dine. They were arriving after the meal and would stay for the rest of the evening. Emma was very happy to be sitting next to Frank during dinner. Mr Weston had told her that his son admired her very much. The young man was certainly paying Emma a lot of attention[52].

During the meal, Emma heard the name of Jane Fairfax spoken. Mrs Cole was talking about her and Emma listened carefully.

'I visited Mrs and Miss Bates this morning,' Mrs Cole was saying. 'Someone has sent Miss Fairfax a piano! It arrived in their house yesterday and no one knows who sent it! It is a beautiful and expensive gift. But they think that it must have come from Colonel Campbell. Miss Fairfax is delighted, of course.

'We have a piano here too,' Mrs Cole went on. 'We hope that Miss Woodhouse will play it later this evening.'

'I should be very pleased to play your piano, Mrs Cole,' Emma replied.

She saw that Frank Churchill was smiling.

'Why are you smiling?' Emma asked, as she smiled too.

'I am happy that Colonel Campbell has given Miss Fairfax such a fine gift,' Frank replied. 'If the Colonel *did* send the piano!'

'Perhaps Mrs Dixon sent it,' Emma said. 'Or Mr Dixon. You told me that Mr Dixon admired Miss Fairfax. He admires her too much, perhaps. I think that is why Miss Fairfax did not go to Ireland. What do you think, Mr Churchill?'

'Well, I think that you may be right, Miss Woodhouse,' Frank replied with a laugh.

'Is it true that Mr Dixon saved Miss Fairfax's life in Weymouth?' Emma asked.

'Yes, he did,' Frank said. 'We were all in a small boat. The wind began to blow strongly and the sea became rough. Miss Fairfax almost fell into the water. Mr Dixon caught her. It all happened very quickly and everyone was very upset.'

Emma was silent for a moment. Then she said, 'This is my opinion. I do not believe that the Campbells sent the piano. I think that it was Mr Dixon's idea. He sent the piano to Miss Fairfax and she knows it. Mr Dixon is in love with Jane Fairfax. That is her secret. What else can it be?'

Frank Churchill smiled at Emma, but he said nothing.

After the meal, the ladies went into the sitting-room. The gentlemen stayed in the dining-room. They drank wine and talked about business, politics and hunting.

A little later, Harriet, Miss Bates and Jane Fairfax arrived. They went and sat with the other ladies.

Harriet looked very pretty and Emma was glad. As usual, Jane Fairfax looked very elegant. She blushed when someone spoke to her about her new piano and Colonel Campbell.

Half an hour later, the gentlemen came into the sitting-room to sit with the ladies. Frank Churchill greeted Miss Bates and Miss Fairfax. Then he walked towards Emma and sat down beside her. Frank Churchill was paying Emma Woodhouse a lot of attention. He thought that she was the most interesting person in the room. Everyone saw this.

'I have been in Highbury for nearly a week,' Frank Churchill said to Emma. 'I have been very happy here. Everyone is so pleasant and I am never bored. When I was in Enscombe, I wanted to go overseas. Now I would be happy to stay with my friends in Highbury for ever!'

'And your friends would be happy too,' Emma replied.

Frank did not answer. He was looking across the room towards Jane Fairfax.

'Is there something wrong?' Emma asked the young man. 'What are you looking at?'

'I am sorry, Miss Woodhouse,' Frank said. 'I was looking at Miss Fairfax's hair. What has she done to it? Those curls[53] look very strange. She did not have curls in Weymouth. Is that hairstyle the latest fashion? I must go and ask her!'

Frank hurried across the room to speak to Jane and Mrs Weston sat down next to Emma.

'I have something very interesting to tell you, Emma,' Mrs Weston said. 'Miss Bates and Miss Fairfax came here in Mr Knightley's carriage and he will take them home again. What do you think about that?'

'I think that Mr Knightley is a very kind man,' Emma said with a smile.

'And I think that he is in love,' Mrs Weston said. 'I think that he is in love with Jane Fairfax. I have made a match between Mr Knightley and Jane Fairfax!'

'That is not possible!' Emma cried. 'I cannot believe that Mr Knightley will ever want to marry. And he will certainly never marry anyone like Jane Fairfax. You are not good at matchmaking, Mrs Weston. I am a better matchmaker. And Mr Knightley will not want Jane Fairfax and Miss Bates at Donwell Abbey. Miss Bates would talk about her *dear* Mrs Knightley all the time! No, I cannot believe that he will marry Jane Fairfax.'

'Then what about her piano?' Mrs Weston said. 'I believe that Mr Knightley sent it. He knows that Jane loves music. I am sure that he is in love with her.'

At that moment, Mrs Cole asked Emma to play their piano. Emma agreed and smiled and she sat down at the instrument.

49

As Emma began to play and sing, Frank Churchill walked over to the piano. He stood beside Emma and sang with her. They sang several songs together and then Emma stood up.

Miss Fairfax took her place.

Jane played and sang much better than Emma and soon Frank was singing with her.

Mr Knightley sat down beside Emma, but he was looking across the room at Jane Fairfax and Frank Churchill.

'Miss Fairfax's voice is not strong,' Mr Knightley said angrily. 'That young man is too fond of the sound of his own voice. He is is making Jane sing too much. I shall ask Miss Bates to stop her.'

Mr Knightley turned to Miss Bates, who was sitting near to them. 'Miss Bates, are you mad?' he said. 'Your niece is singing far too much. She will hurt her throat. Please stop her!'

Miss Bates was worried about Jane too. She hurried across to the piano and spoke to her niece quietly. Jane nodded and stood up.

After this, Mrs Weston started to play the piano and the dancing began.

Frank Churchill walked with Emma to the first dancing position[54] and other couples soon joined them. Emma looked at Mr Knightley. Would he ask Jane Fairfax to dance with him? No, he did not.

Emma was pleased. Mr Knightley was certainly not in love with Miss Fairfax!

There was only time for two dances and then everyone prepared to go home. Frank took Emma to her carriage.

'I am glad there was no time for more dances,' Frank said. 'I would not have enjoyed dancing with Miss Fairfax, after dancing with you!'

Emma was pleased that she had gone to the Coles' dinner party. The evening had made her think about a lot of things.

Frank Churchill walked with Emma to the first dancing position.

Did Jane Fairfax have feelings for Frank Churchill? Emma did not think so. But she knew that Jane's playing and singing were far better than her own.

7

The Piano

The next morning, Emma sat down at her own piano to practise. But after a few minutes, Harriet came into the room and Emma stopped playing.

Harriet wanted to go to Mrs Ford's shop and buy some cloth. She was going to make a new dress. Emma agreed to go into Highbury with her. She did not want Harriet to meet the Martins again when she was alone in the village.

It took Harriet a long time to choose the cloth. Emma stood by the door of the shop and looked up and down the street. Suddenly she saw Mrs Weston and Frank Churchill walking together on the other side of the street. When they saw Emma, they crossed the street to speak to her.

'We are going to the Bateses' house, to hear the new piano,' Mrs Weston said. 'And then we were planning to go to Hartfield to see you.'

'Perhaps you can visit the Bateses by yourself,' Frank said to Mrs Weston. 'I will go back to Hartfield with Miss Woodhouse and wait for you there.'

'Do come with me, Frank,' Mrs Weston said. 'Miss Bates will be so happy to see you.'

Frank agreed and Emma went back into the shop. She helped Harriet choose the cloth and some ribbon[55]. At last, Harriet decided what she wanted. Mrs Ford promised to send the cloth and ribbon in a parcel to Hartfield.

As Emma and Harriet were leaving the shop, Mrs Weston and Miss Bates came in. As usual, Miss Bates began talking at once.

'My dear Miss Woodhouse!' she cried. 'Please come across the street to my house and sit with us for a little time. You must hear the new piano. I — we should so like to hear your opinion of it. You play so well yourself, Miss Woodhouse. Mr Churchill said that I should ask you — yes, Mr Churchill. He is repairing my mother's spectacles[56]. She broke them this morning! Is that not clever of Mr Churchill — so kind ...'

Still talking, Miss Bates led the others out of the shop and across the street to the house where she lived. They walked up the stairs and into the little sitting-room.

Old Mrs Bates was asleep in a chair by the fire and Frank was sitting at a table. Jane was standing by her new piano, looking at a book of music.

Frank looked up from the pair of spectacles that he was holding and smiled.

'You see, Miss Woodhouse, I am being useful,' he said. 'Look. I have repaired Mrs Bates's spectacles. And now that you are all here, perhaps Miss Fairfax will play for us.'

Jane sat down at the piano and began to play. Everyone agreed that the piano was a very good one.

'Colonel Campbell, or someone, chose very well,' Frank said softly. Then he said in a louder voice, 'I wonder if your friends in Ireland are thinking of you now, Miss Fairfax. I am sure that Colonel Campbell would like to see you now with his gift!'

'I am not sure that Colonel Campbell sent the piano,' Jane said, very quietly.

Frank walked across the room and stood beside her.

'Please play one of the tunes[57] that we danced to last night,' he said.

As Jane began to play, the young man smiled.

'That tune brings back happy memories[58]!' Frank said. 'We heard that tune in Weymouth too.'

Jane blushed and she stopped playing at once.

'Please do not stop!' Frank Churchill said. 'Here is a book of Irish tunes. They were sent with the piano, I believe. Play one of these tunes, Miss Fairfax. Everything has been chosen so carefully. These gifts were sent with real friendship, even love.'

Emma looked at Jane and was surprised. Jane was smiling. She had understood Frank Churchill's words very well. He was talking about Mr Dixon – a married man.

Emma understood too. Mr Dixon had sent the piano. Mr Dixon had married Miss Campbell, but he loved beautiful, perfect Miss Fairfax.

'That is her secret,' Emma thought. 'That is the secret that Jane is hiding. I am sure that is the truth!'

At that moment, Miss Bates looked out of the window.

'Oh, there is Mr Knightley riding by on his horse!' she cried. 'I will go into mother's room and call to him.'

The rooms were very small and everyone could hear Miss Bates as she spoke to Mr Knightley.

'Thank you so much for sending your carriage for us last night,' she said through the open window. 'Do come in and see us all.'

'How is your niece, Miss Bates?' Mr Knightley asked. 'I hope that Miss Fairfax is well.'

'Jane is very well, thank you. But do come up and see for yourself. Miss Woodhouse and Miss Smith are here.'

'Well, just for five minutes, perhaps,' Mr Knightley said.

'Mrs Weston and Mr Frank Churchill are here too,' Miss Bates went on. 'They will be very happy to see you.'

'Then your sitting-room is full enough,' Mr Knightley said quickly. 'I will visit you another day and hear Miss

'That tune brings back happy memories!'

Fairfax play then. Good morning to you, Miss Bates.' Then he bowed politely and rode on.

———

Frank Churchill had enjoyed dancing at the Coles and he now wanted to dance again. He wanted to dance at a ball. Soon he talked about nothing else.

One evening, when Emma and her father were at Randalls, Frank had an idea.

'Our next ball can be here!' he said. 'Mrs Weston can play the piano for us again. We can invite the same young people who danced before. We could invite ten couples.'

Mr and Mrs Weston were interested in Frank's idea, but Emma saw a problem.

'This room is not big enough for ten couples,' she said. ' It will be too crowded.'

Frank thought for a moment and then he stood up. He walked towards the door and opened it.

'Look,' he said. 'This door is opposite the one across the passage. If both doors are open, we can use these two rooms for dancing!'

Mr Woodhouse was very upset at this idea.

'It would be very dangerous to have all those doors open,' he said. 'There will be too many draughts. Emma would catch a cold and so would poor little Harriet. Please, my dear Mrs Weston, do not agree to such an idea!'

Then he added more quietly, 'That young man is very thoughtless. There is a bad draught here. Those doors should be closed at once!'

Mrs Weston frowned at Frank and he closed the doors. No one said anything more about the ball that evening.

The next morning, Frank was at Hartfield to talk about the ball again. The young man smiled happily at Mr Woodhouse and Emma.

'You said that Randalls was too small for a ball, Miss

Woodhouse, and you were right,' Frank said. 'My father has had a better idea. We will have the ball at the Crown Inn in Highbury! What do you think about that?'

'It is a very good idea,' Emma said. 'Do you not agree with me, Papa?'

Mr Woodhouse shook his head sadly. 'Rooms in inns are always damp,' the old man said. 'A dance at the Crown Inn would be very dangerous. Everyone would catch a cold!'

'No, sir. The rooms at the Crown are larger than here at Randalls,' Frank Churchill replied. 'So we would not have to open the windows in the inn when the room becomes hot.'

'Open windows when young people are dancing!' Mr Woodhouse cried. 'I cannot believe what you are saying, Mr Churchill. That is very dangerous. Everyone would be very cold. They would become ill.'

Emma spoke quietly to her father.

'No one is going to open any windows,' she said. 'The Crown Inn will be a better place for a ball, Papa. It will be better for the carriage horses too. They will not have so far to go.'

'Well, that is true,' Mr Woodhouse said. 'But we must make sure that the rooms are not damp.'

'Papa, our dear Mrs Weston will be arranging everything. You know how careful she is.'

'You are right,' Mr Woodhouse replied more happily. 'Mrs Weston always looked after us well when she was at Hartfield.'

'My father and Mrs Weston are at the Crown Inn now,' Frank said to Emma. 'They need your opinion, Miss Woodhouse. Please let me take you there at once.'

Everyone soon agreed. The ballroom at the Crown was a good size and there was another, smaller room. This room could be used by the older people who wanted to play cards.

'The paint in these rooms is not very clean,' Mrs Weston said.

'That will not be a problem,' Mr Weston said. 'We shall be dancing in the evening. Candles will light the room. No one will see a little dirt.'

Mrs Weston and Emma smiled at each other. Men never worried about things like dirt!

'We shall have everything cleaned,' Mrs Weston said.

'We need a supper-room,' Emma said. 'This small room is not big enough.'

'There is another, larger room along this passage,' Mr Weston called. 'Come and look. It is not too far away and there are no draughts.'

'I wonder what our guests would like,' Mrs Weston said. 'We need another opinion.'

'I know! We need Miss Bates!' Frank Churchill said. 'I shall go and fetch her.'

'Bring her niece too,' Mr Weston said. 'She has more sense than her aunt.'

Frank hurried away. Mrs Weston and Emma walked through the rooms and talked about the arrangements for the ball. When Frank returned with Miss Bates and Miss Fairfax, the ladies soon agreed about everything: tables, chairs, food, lights, the musicians and the music that they would play.

Before they all left the inn, Emma promised that she would dance the first two dances with Frank Churchill. Mr Weston looked at his wife and smiled.

'My dear, Frank has asked Emma if she will dance the first two dances with him,' he said quietly. 'I knew that he would ask her.'

Later, Emma thought about Frank Churchill. 'He is a very determined young man,' Emma said to herself. 'He knows what he wants and he gets it. If I were thinking of marrying him, I would be a little worried. But he is my friend. If he is selfish, I do not care.'

———

The plans for the ball began at once. The Churchills agreed that Frank could stay in Highbury for another week. Even Jane Fairfax became excited.

'Oh, Miss Woodhouse,' Jane said. 'I am delighted that we are having a ball. I hope that nothing stops our plans!'

Mr Knightley did not feel the same way. He never danced and he hated the idea of a ball. Emma decided that Mrs Weston was wrong. Mr Knightley could not be interested in Jane Fairfax.

And then a letter arrived from Enscombe in Yorkshire. Mrs Churchill was ill. Frank Churchill had to return home at once. There would be no ball. Frank sent Emma a note and then went to see her at Hartfield.

'I have been so happy these last two weeks,' Frank said. 'But now everything has changed! There can be no ball and I cannot stay in Highbury. I have to leave this morning – at once! I shall hear about you all from Mrs Weston's letters, of course.'

'Do you not even have time to say goodbye to Miss Bates and her niece?' Emma asked with a sad smile.

'I called there before I came here,' Frank said quickly. 'Miss Bates was out and I could not wait for her to return. But I think that you must understand, Miss Woodhouse. You understand things so quickly. I had to call there, and to see *you* at Hartfield too ...'

'Of course you had to see Miss Bates,' Emma said quickly.

Frank did not answer. In a few minutes he had bowed, shaken Emma's hand and was gone.

'Am I in love with Frank Churchill?' Emma asked herself. 'I am sure that he is in love with *me*. I shall never marry, of course, but his feelings for me are very strong. Perhaps I do love him a little ...'

So Frank Churchill left Highbury and everyone except Mr Knightley was very unhappy.

Emma went to visit Jane Fairfax that afternoon, but Jane was feeling unwell. She had a very bad headache[59] and could not see Emma.

Then news came to Highbury that Mr Elton was married. He would soon be returning with his new bride. Everyone in Highbury began talking about Mr and Mrs Elton.

In a few days, Mr Frank Churchill was almost forgotten, except by his friends.

Harriet was very upset when she heard the news about Mr Elton's marriage. The young girl had not expected the vicar's marriage to happen so soon. She wept for many hours and Emma listened to her friend talking about her love for Mr Elton.

'Poor Harriet, she has a warm loving heart,' Emma said to herself. 'She is so different from cold Jane Fairfax!'

8

Mrs Elton

It was spring. The people of Highbury saw Mrs Elton for the first time in the church. Emma was one of the first people to call on Mr Elton's wife at the vicarage and she took Harriet with her.

Emma remembered the last time that she had been in the vicar's house. Harriet sat silently. Her face was pale. She remembered too.

The visit was short, but Emma's first opinion of Mrs Elton was not good. Mrs Elton was wearing an elegant dress, but she herself was not elegant. She was vulgar[60]. She was not very polite and she talked too much.

Mr Elton was not happy to see Emma again and he said very little. His manners were not those of a real gentleman.

The Eltons soon came to call at Hartfield. Harriet was not visiting the house, so Mr Woodhouse talked to Mr Elton. Emma was able to watch Mrs Elton carefully.

Emma soon made up her mind about Mrs Elton. She was a vain[61] and silly woman who only thought of money and polite society.

'Hartfield is very like my brother-in-law's house, Maple Grove,' Mrs Elton said, walking about. 'This room is like the smallest sitting-room at Maple Grove. And the staircase here is exactly the same. I have spent so many happy months at Maple Grove! I did not expect to find a house like Maple Grove in Highbury. I think that the garden here is much the same too, but smaller, of course. I feel very comfortable here at Hartfield, Miss Woodhouse, very comfortable.'

'I am pleased to hear that,' Emma said.

Mrs Elton walked to the window and looked through it.

'Yes, I was right,' she said with a smile. 'The garden here *is* like the garden at Maple Grove.

'I am sure that the country around Highbury is very fine too,' Mrs Elton went on. 'Mr Suckling, my brother-in-law, will be visiting us in the spring. He has a very large carriage and will drive us to the most beautiful places. I am sure that you and your friends enjoy driving around the neighbourhood too.'

'The people of Highbury are usually happy to stay at home,' Emma said quietly.

Mrs Elton looked at Mr Woodhouse and sighed.

'I understand that your father's health keeps him at home,' Mrs Elton said sadly. ' Why does he not go to Bath? I am sure that a visit to Bath would be good for him. And for you too, Miss Woodhouse. I could give you introductions[62] to the very best people there!'

61

Emma was very angry but she did not let Mrs Elton see her feelings. She decided to talk about something else.

'I believe that you are interested in music, Mrs Elton,' Emma said with a smile. 'We enjoy good music in Highbury.'

'Oh, yes, I cannot live without music,' Mrs Elton replied. 'But I am a married woman now, Miss Woodhouse. I may not have time for music.'

Emma had no answer to that and soon Mrs Elton began talking again.

'Mr Elton and I visited Randalls earlier,' she said. 'The Westons seem to be very pleasant people. Mrs Weston was your governess, I believe. She has very good manners. But who do you think came in when we were there, Miss Woodhouse?'

Emma did not know.

'It was Knightley[63]!' Mrs Elton said happily. 'My husband's friend, Knightley! I like Knightley very much. He is a real gentleman. I shall invite him to dine at the vicarage.'

It was time for the Eltons to leave. Emma was delighted to see them go.

'What a vulgar woman!' Emma said to herself when she was alone. '*She* thinks that Mr Knightley is a gentleman! She calls him Knightley! Not Mr Knightley – but *Knightley*! And she thinks that dear Mrs Weston has *very good manners*! Mr Elton has chosen a very unsuitable wife. He has made a bad choice. I wonder what Frank Churchill would think about Mrs Elton. He will certainly laugh at her!'

Then she thought for a second and smiled. 'I am always thinking about Frank Churchill. I must be a little in love with him ...'

Emma did not change her opinion of Mrs Elton. And Mrs Elton no longer tried to please Emma Woodhouse. When they met again, Mrs Elton had changed. She was very unfriendly.

'I like Knightley very much. He is a real gentleman.'

Mr and Mrs Elton were both unkind to Harriet and that made Emma angry too.

Mrs Elton had decided that her best friend in Highbury would be Jane Fairfax.

'What a delightful girl dear Jane is!' Mrs Elton said to Emma one day. 'She is so charming and she plays and sings so well. But the poor girl is too quiet. I shall introduce Jane to all my friends.

'I understand that she is going to be a governess,' Mrs Elton went on. 'I must find the very best family for her. I know so many good families who need a governess, Miss Woodhouse. I shall soon find a good position somewhere for my poor, dear Jane.'

Emma did not understand or like Jane, but she began to feel sorry for her.

———

Jane Fairfax had now been in Highbury for three months. The Campbells and the Dixons had decided to stay in Ireland until the summer. They invited Jane to stay with them there, but she refused.

One day Mrs Weston visited Hartfield. Mr Knightley was also there.

'Why does Jane Fairfax stay in Highbury?' Emma asked Mrs Weston. 'She cannot enjoy going to the vicarage.'

'Perhaps it is better than always being with Mrs and Miss Bates,' Mrs Weston replied.

'You are right, Mrs Weston,' Mr Knightley said. 'If Jane had other friends, she might not have chosen Mrs Elton.'

As he spoke, Mr Knightley looked at Emma.

'At least Mrs Elton is kind to Jane Fairfax,' he added.

'We all know how much you admire Jane Fairfax,' Emma said quickly.

'Yes, I do admire her,' Mr Knightley said. 'I admire Jane Fairfax very much.'

'Be careful that your admiration does not become something else,' Emma said with a laugh.

'I understand you,' Mr Knightley said. 'But Miss Fairfax would not marry me if I asked her. And I am not going to ask her. Do not start matchmaking again, Emma. Remember what happened with Harriet Smith.'

'I am not matchmaking,' Emma replied. 'I do not want you to marry Jane Fairfax. I do not want you to marry anyone, Mr Knightley.'

Mr Knightley smiled. 'Jane Fairfax is very charming, but she is not perfect,' he said. 'She keeps her thoughts to herself. I like people to say what they think. Jane is a woman of strong feelings, but she is very reserved. I admire her, but that is all.'

After Mr Knightley had left, Mrs Weston looked at Emma and laughed.

'Mr Knightley is very sure that he does not love Jane,' Mrs Weston said. 'Perhaps he is too sure. We shall see!'

9

Hartfield

Mr Elton and his new wife received many invitations from the people of Highbury. Emma decided that she must ask them to dinner at Hartfield. As only six people were invited to the meal, Mr Woodhouse was quite happy. He enjoyed having dinner with a few friends in his own home.

The Eltons, the Westons and Mr Knightley all accepted Emma's invitation to dinner. Harriet did not want to see the

Eltons, so Emma did not invite her to Hartfield. She invited Jane Fairfax.

At Christmas, John Knightley had promised to bring his two oldest sons to Hartfield in the spring. The boys would stay with their aunt and grandfather for a few weeks.

John Knightley and his young sons came for their visit on the same day as the dinner party. They arrived early in the morning. John planned to stay in Hartfield for the night and return to London early the following day.

Mr Woodhouse was very upset when his son-in-law arrived. There were now going to be nine people at dinner, not eight. Mr Woodhouse was uncomfortable in large groups of people. They made him feel unwell.

Then Mr Weston sent a message. He had to go to London on business and could not come to dine. There would be only eight people at dinner, after all. Mr Woodhouse was happy again.

At four o'clock, all the guests for the dinner party arrived. The Eltons brought Jane with them in their carriage. Mrs Elton looked very elegant in a dress made of lace and a long necklace of pearls[64].

John Knightley did not like meeting strangers, but he had met Jane Fairfax many times in London. He was pleased to see Jane at Hartfield. She was a quiet, clever girl and John Knightley enjoyed her company. They were soon talking together happily.

'I hope that you did not get wet this morning, before breakfast, Miss Fairfax,' John Knightley said with a smile. 'I saw you when I was walking in the village with my boys. It was raining heavily.'

'I only went to the post office,' Jane answered. 'I fetch the letters every morning. A walk before breakfast is good for me.'

John Knightley smiled. 'We always like receiving letters

'I saw you when I was walking in the village with my boys.'

when we are young,' he said. 'I am older than you and I do not like letters so much now.'

'You are talking about business letters, Mr Knightley,' Jane said quickly. 'I was talking about letters from friends. Many of my friends live far away. Your family and all your friends are close to you. You do not need letters from them.'

'My dear Miss Fairfax, I am ten years older than you,' John Knightley replied. 'I am sure that in ten years' time, things will be different. You will have a loving family of your own.'

Jane's eyes filled with tears. 'Thank you,' she said quietly.

Other people heard this conversation. Soon everybody was talking about Jane's walk to the post office in the rain. Old Mr Woodhouse was very worried when he heard this. He spoke to Jane in his usual kind way.

'Young ladies should not walk in the rain,' Mr Woodhouse said. 'Miss Fairfax, you must take care of yourself. I hope that you changed your stockings[65] when you returned to your aunt's house. Wet stockings are very dangerous.'

Then the kind old man added, 'I am so pleased to see you here, Miss Fairfax, and my daughter is too.'

Mrs Elton was not as polite as Mr Woodhouse.

'You were walking in the rain?' she cried. 'What a silly girl you are! We cannot let you do that again, can we, Mrs Weston? The servant who gets our letters from the post office can get yours too, Jane.'

'You are very kind, Mrs Elton,' Jane said. 'But I enjoy my morning walk to the post office. I must get my own letters.'

Mrs Elton laughed and shook her head. Jane turned away and began to speak to John Knightley again.

Emma was listening with interest. It was clear that Jane's letters were very important to her. Did they come from Ireland? Had Jane received a letter that morning? Had she received a letter from Mr Dixon, perhaps?

Emma had noticed that Jane was looking much happier than usual. Emma smiled at her and the two beautiful girls walked into the dining-room together. They sat beside each other during dinner. Mr Knightley was very pleased to see that Emma and Jane were becoming friends.

After dinner, Mrs Elton sat next to Jane and began talking to her in her loud voice.

'I am getting worried about you, Jane,' Mrs Elton said. 'It is already April and you plan to be a governess by June! Have you had any answers to your enquiries?'

'I have not made any enquiries,' Jane said. 'The Campbells will be in London by June and I must spend some time with them.'

'But all the best positions go to people who make enquiries early!' Mrs Elton cried. 'I shall tell my friends all about you. You are so clever and well educated! I must find you a position with a very good family. I know that you are shy[66], but I can help you, do not worry!'

'Thank you,' Jane said quietly. 'But for the next few months, I shall be staying in Highbury.'

At that moment, everyone was surprised when Mr Weston came into the room. 'I got back from London an hour ago,' he said.

'I bring you good news, Anne,' he said to his wife. 'It has come in a letter. Read it, my dear, and you too, Emma!'

Mrs Weston took the letter and smiled as she read it. It was from Frank Churchill. He was writing to say that Mrs Churchill was tired of her home in Yorkshire. The Churchills were planning to stay in London for a few months. So Frank would be staying only sixteen miles from Highbury! Mrs Weston was as happy as her husband.

Emma was not sure about her own feelings – would she be happy to see Frank Churchill again? She would have to think about that.

Mr Weston looked around for someone to talk to about Frank. Jane Fairfax was having a conversation with John Knightley. His brother, Mr Knightley, was frowning. It was clear that the news about the Churchills had not pleased him.

So Mr Weston sat down next to Mrs Elton and began talking to her.

'I hope that I shall soon be able to introduce my son to you,' Mr Weston said with a smile. 'His name is Frank Churchill.'

'That name is very well known in Highbury,' Mrs Elton replied. 'Mr Elton and I will be happy to invite the young man to the vicarage.'

That was what Mr Weston wanted to hear and he was soon telling Mrs Elton all about his son.

Frank Churchill arrived in Highbury in late spring. He had been away for two months. His visit was very short, but he called on his father and stepmother at Randalls as well as the Woodhouses at Hartfield.

Frank greeted Emma warmly. But he greeted her as a friend. She could not see any signs of love. Did he love her, or had she been mistaken? Frank stayed at Hartfield for only fifteen minutes, then he hurried away to call on other friends.

Then Frank left Highbury suddenly and returned to London for ten days. When he came back to Highbury again, he brought more news. Mrs Churchill did not like London after all. It was too noisy. The Churchills were moving to Richmond – a village near London – in the early summer. They planned to stay there for the months of May and June. Richmond was a very quiet place, only twelve miles away from Highbury. The Westons were very pleased. And there was more exciting news for the people of Highbury.

Frank Churchill had not forgotten about the plans for a

ball at the Crown Inn. He told the Westons to choose the day and make all the arrangements. The young people of Highbury were all delighted.

10

The Ball

It was the day of the ball and the weather was wet. Frank Churchill had arrived at the Westons' house, Randalls, before dinner. He heard that everything was ready. All the arrangements for the ball had been made.

There was no time for him to visit the Woodhouses at Hartfield that day. Emma and Frank would meet at the ball itself.

'There will be a crowd of people there,' Emma thought. 'That will be better. I shall be able to hide my feelings about Frank.'

Mr Woodhouse was not going to the ball. Emma had invited his old friends, Mrs Bates and Mrs Goddard to Hartfield. The three old people would enjoy a quiet dinner and a game of cards together.

Emma and Harriet arrived at the Crown Inn before most of the other guests. The Westons and Frank Churchill were already there. The friends saw that everything was ready.

Although it was May, it was a cold evening and a warm fire was burning in the fireplace in the ballroom. It was still raining outside, but inside the inn, all the rooms were warm and comfortable. In the card-room and supper-room there were tables and chairs. There were many lighted candles everywhere. The musicians were ready to play. Everything was perfect. Everything was ready for the Westons' guests.

Frank smiled at Emma, but he did not stay near her for long. He was very restless. He hurried to the door each time that he heard the sound of a carriage outside.

The Eltons were the first couple to arrive. Mrs Elton's dress and her necklace of pearls were very elegant.

'Where are Miss Bates and Miss Fairfax?' Mr Weston said. 'I thought that they were coming with you, Mrs Elton!'

Mrs Elton had forgotten to call at the Bateses' house and bring Miss Fairfax and Miss Bates with her.

Immediately, Mr Weston sent his own carriage to bring the ladies to the inn. Frank went to the door of the inn to wait for them. He took an umbrella[67] with him.

'Your son is a fine young man, Mr Weston,' Mrs Elton said. 'He is so well mannered and so handsome too! You must be very proud of him!'

Mr Weston was always happy to hear praise of his son and he agreed with everything that Mrs Elton said.

Frank himself soon returned, bringing with him Miss Bates and Jane Fairfax.

Miss Bates came into the room smiling and talking as usual.

'It was so kind of Mr Weston to send his carriage!' she cried. 'No, we are not wet — just a little rain — Mr Churchill had an umbrella. What bright candles! What a beautiful room! I never thought — Yes, my mother is well. She is with Mr Woodhouse. She is wearing her new warm shawl. It was a present from Mrs Dixon. She bought it in Weymouth. They are all so kind. Mr Churchill is so kind too — bringing an umbrella for us. Oh, dear Miss Woodhouse, how fine you look! Do you like Jane's hairstyle? She arranged it herself. She is so clever. No coffee, thank you — perhaps some tea. Oh, thank you. Yes, I shall sit down — here in this chair. Then I shall be out of the way …'

Frank went and stood next to Emma. Mrs Elton walked across the room to where Jane Fairfax was standing. She began to praise Jane's hairstyle and her dress.

'And what do you think of *my* dress?' Mrs Elton went on. 'I believe my pearls are the finest in the room. I hear that Mr Frank Churchill is a very good dancer. Well, we shall see.'

'Do you like Mrs Elton?' Emma asked Frank very quietly.

'I do not like her at all,' Frank replied.

'But she is praising you,' Emma said with a smile. 'Mrs Elton thinks that you are very handsome!'

Frank did not answer. He was looking round the room for Mr Weston.

'Where is my father?' Frank said. 'When are we going to begin dancing?'

Mr Weston walked across the ballroom to speak to his son.

'Mrs Elton must have a dancing-partner. She will expect you to dance with her first[68], Frank,' he said.

Frank shook his head. 'No, Father. I am sorry. I have made a promise to Miss Woodhouse. We are dancing the first dance together,' he said. 'You can be Mrs Elton's partner, Father. You can lead the dance with her. She will like that.'

Several couples were now standing ready and the dancing began. Mr Weston stood first in the line with Mrs Elton. Emma and Frank Churchill were next to them. Emma was feeling very happy. She knew that she was well dressed and elegant. And she knew that she and Mr Frank Churchill danced well together.

Emma saw Mr Knightley standing and talking to some other guests.

'It is a pity that Mr Knightley is not dancing,' she thought. 'He looks so tall and handsome. He is the most handsome man in the room, after Frank Churchill.'

Harriet Smith was not dancing either and Emma felt sorry

for her. Mrs Weston did too. Mr Elton was walking about the room without a dancing-partner and Mrs Weston spoke to him.

'You are not dancing, Mr Elton,' she said. 'Shall I find you a partner for the next dance?'

Mr Elton smiled. 'I would be happy to dance with *you*, Mrs Weston,' he said, politely.

'I do not dance,' Mrs Weston said with a laugh. 'But here is Miss Harriet Smith, a very pretty girl without a partner for the next dance. She would be happy to dance with you, I am sure.'

'Thank you, thank you, but I do not need a partner,' Mr Elton said quickly. 'I am an old married man and my dancing days are over!'

Mr Elton turned away from Harriet and went to sit down.

Emma was angry at Mr Elton's rudeness and she felt very sorry for Harriet. Then to Emma's surprise, Mr Knightley walked over to Harriet, bowed, and asked her to dance.

Harriet stood up, smiling happily.

Emma was pleased. Mr Knightley had shown kindness to her friend. Emma was also pleased to see that Mr Knightley danced very well. She smiled happily as the musicians played another tune.

Some time later, it was time for supper. The delicious food was put on tables in the supper-room and people began to walk along the passage. They were laughing and talking.

Miss Bates walked with Jane and of course, Miss Bates was talking too.

'Jane, dear Jane, please put on this shawl — the passage may be cold. Oh, Mr Churchill — there you are! Jane, dear, Mr Churchill has helped you. You are so kind, Mr Churchill. Jane, you will be warmer now. I am so pleased to watch the dancing. Yes, Jane dear — Mr Woodhouse sent Grandmamma back from Hartfield in his carriage. I ran home to help her

Mr Knightley walked over to Harriet, bowed, and asked her to dance.

into bed. No one missed me — and here I am, back again! Grandmamma had such a good evening with Mr Woodhouse. Dinner, cards and then tea. Oh, thank you, Mr Churchill — you are kind to help Jane and myself! Oh, but Mrs Elton must go to the supper table first. She is wearing a *very* elegant dress! Here are two steps, take care, Jane — oh, just one step! Your grandmamma was a little disappointed, dear. There was her favourite food at dinner — but Mr Woodhouse sent it back to the kitchen. He said that it was not cooked enough. Well, look at all this delicious food — we must tell Grandmamma all about it. Thank you, thank you, Mr Churchill — you have given me too much food on this plate. It looks delicious …'

———

After supper, Mr Knightley spoke to Emma about Mr Elton's rudeness to Harriet Smith.

'The Eltons are your enemies, Emma,' Mr Knightley said. 'I think that you wanted Mr Elton to marry Harriet. Am I right?'

'Yes. I did want Mr Elton and Harriet to marry. And the Eltons cannot forgive me,' Emma replied.

'Well, I do not agree with your matchmaking, but Harriet was the better choice for Mr Elton,' Mr Knightley said. 'Harriet Smith is a sweet kind girl. These are good qualities, but Mrs Elton has no good qualities at all.'

Soon Mr Weston was asking everyone to begin dancing again.

'Come along, Emma!' he cried. 'Show everyone what to do.'

'I am ready,' Emma said happily.

'Who are you going to dance with?' Mr Knightley asked her.

'With you, if you will ask me,' Emma replied with a smile.

'Will you, Emma?'

'Of course I will, Mr Knightley. You have shown me that you can dance,' Emma said, smiling. 'We are not brother and sister[69], are we, Mr Knightley? We are very good friends.'

'Brother and sister? Certainly not!' he replied.

11

Harriet is in Love Again

The next morning, Emma thought about the ball as she walked in the garden at Hartfield. She decided that it had gone well. She had enjoyed dancing with Mr Knightley and she was pleased that he had danced with Harriet.

Emma had decided that Frank Churchill was not in love with her. Or perhaps he did love her – but only a little. The summer would be a happy and interesting time.

Emma turned to walk back into the house and saw two people coming towards her – Harriet and Mr Frank Churchill.

Harriet was crying and holding Mr Churchill's arm. Emma took them into the house, and made Harriet sit down. And then the poor girl fainted[70]!

Frank Churchill quickly explained what had happened.

Harriet and another pupil from Mrs Goddard's school had been walking along a quiet little road. They had met a group of gypsies[71], who started asking the girls for money.

The other girl was very frightened. She screamed and ran away. But Harriet was too tired after the ball. She did not run. The gypsies were soon all around her. They shouted at her and asked for money. Harriet gave them a coin, but they wanted more and poor Harriet became very frightened.

At that moment, Frank Churchill came along the road and saw everything. He was carrying a stick and very soon, the gypsies were as frightened as Harriet had been. They ran away and Frank had brought Harriet to Hartfield.

Frank Churchill could not stay after Emma had heard the story. He had to return to the Churchills in Richmond.

Harriet spent the day at Hartfield with Emma and was soon feeling much better.

What an adventure for Harriet Smith! She had been badly frightened and then rescued by handsome Frank Churchill! Emma did not want her father to hear the story. But soon everyone in Highbury, including her father, knew about it.

Harriet was not hurt, only frightened. Emma began to think about Harriet and Mr Frank Churchill. Was it possible that they could love each other? Would they be a good match for each other?

A few days later, Harriet returned to Hartfield. She had a little parcel in her hand.

'Miss Woodhouse, if you have time, I have something to tell you,' Harriet said. 'I have been very silly. I want to tell you everything.'

Emma was very surprised and she asked Harriet to go on.

'I do not care if I meet Mr Elton or not,' Harriet said. 'I wanted to tell you that. And I think that Mrs Elton is very bad tempered. I do not like her at all. I have been very silly, Miss Woodhouse, but my feelings have changed. I want to show you that I no longer love Mr Elton. Look.'

Harriet slowly untied the parcel. Inside the paper there was a little box. Harriet lifted the lid of the box.

Emma looked inside it and was surprised.

'All I can see is a piece of plaster[72] and the end of an old pencil,' Emma said slowly. 'What have they to do with Mr Elton, Harriet?'

'Surely you remember, Miss Woodhouse,' Harriet said. 'One day, Mr Elton cut his finger and I gave him some plaster. There was a little piece of the plaster which he did not use. He held the piece in his hand for a time and here it is. This was his pencil, but it was too small and he threw it away. Later on, I picked it up and kept it.

'Look, Miss Woodhouse, I am going to throw the pencil and the plaster onto the fire. There!' she said, throwing them into the flames, 'That is the end of my love for Mr Elton.

'I shall never marry now,' Harriet added. 'The man whom I love will never know my feelings. I admire him so much, but he will never know. I shall never tell him of my love.'

'Tell him? Tell *who*, Harriet?' Emma cried. '*Who* are you talking about?' She was becoming tired of this word game.

'As soon as I saw him coming towards me, I knew ...' Harriet began. 'He is a real gentleman. He was so kind to me. I shall never forget it. My feelings have changed so quickly. But they will never change again, Miss Woodhouse, never.'

However, when Emma asked Harriet the gentleman's name, her friend only shook her head and smiled. She would not answer.

'I think that I understand,' Emma said, with a kind smile. 'But I shall not give you any advice this time. Do what you feel is right, my dear Harriet. You have made a good choice.'

———

It was now June. Jane Fairfax was still in Highbury and she was planning to stay for another two months.

Mr Frank Churchill was often at Randalls and everyone liked the young man – everyone except Mr Knightley.

Most people in Highbury thought that there would be a match between Frank Churchill and Emma Woodhouse. But Emma herself hoped that Frank was falling in love with Harriet. And she thought that Harriet was in love with Frank Churchill.

Mr Knightley had a different thought. He believed that Frank and Jane were more than friends. Mr Knightley had seen Frank Churchill looking at Jane Fairfax. He thought that Frank Churchill had a secret.

One warm evening, Mr Knightley was walking with Emma and Harriet in the main street of Highbury. They saw Mr and Mrs Weston and Frank Churchill, who had met Miss Bates and Jane.

Emma invited all her friends to come to Hartfield for tea with herself and Mr Woodhouse.

'My father would be delighted to see you all,' Emma said. 'A meeting of good friends in his own house is just the kind of surprise that he likes.'

They all agreed to come to Emma's home. As they walked towards the gates of Hartfield, Dr Perry rode by on his horse.

Frank looked surprised. 'Did you not tell me that Dr Perry was buying his own carriage?' he said to Mrs Weston.

'No, I did not,' Mrs Weston said.

'But you told me so in one of your letters!' Frank said. 'Mrs Perry told her husband that they should buy more horses and a carriage. Do you not remember?'

'I have never heard of it before.'

Frank laughed. 'I must have dreamt it then,' he said. 'I am always dreaming of Highbury when I am away! But why should I dream about Dr Perry?'

'Oh dear!' Miss Bates cried, 'I think that I can explain. It was not a dream at all, Mr Churchill. Dr Perry did plan to buy a carriage in the spring, but it was a secret. Mrs Perry told my mother and my mother told us. Do you not remember, Jane?'

Jane Fairfax was at the back of the group and did not hear her aunt's question.

'Oh. Well, perhaps I told someone else,' Miss Bates went on. 'I do talk a lot, I know. I must have told someone about the carriage.'

Mr Knightley looked at Frank. The young man had heard Miss Bates's words. Now Frank was looking at Jane and trying not to laugh. Jane did not notice that Frank was looking at her. She walked on into the house.

The visitors were soon sitting at the large dining-table at Hartfield and drinking tea. Frank sat down next to Emma.

Frank picked up a little wooden box that was on the table and opened it. The box belonged to Emma's young nephews. Inside it, there were letters of the alphabet which were made of wood.

'Let us play a word game with these letters,' Frank said to Emma.

As he spoke, Frank took a few letters from the box and put them on the table. Then he made a word and pushed the letters across the table towards Jane Fairfax. Jane soon guessed the word, but she pushed the letters away again.

Harriet picked them up and tried to make the word with Mr Knightley's help.

'MISTAKE!' Harriet cried. 'The word is MISTAKE.'

Frank laughed, but Jane blushed and shook her head.

Mr Knightley did not know what to think. Was Frank laughing at Jane and at Emma too?

Frank pushed another five letters towards Emma and smiled. She quickly made them into a word and then moved the letters about again.

'Shall I ask Jane to make this word?' Frank said quietly to Emma.

'No, no. You must not,' Emma replied, but Frank had already pushed the five letters towards Jane.

Mr Knightley saw that the letters made the name, DIXON.

Jane looked very unhappy.

'People's names cannot be used in the game, Mr Churchill,' she said. Then she turned towards Miss Bates and spoke to her quietly.

Miss Bates stood up. 'Yes, my dear Jane, you are right,' she said. 'It is time to go.'

Jane stood up too, and put on her shawl. Frank pushed some more letters towards Jane, but she turned away. Mr Knightley did not see if Frank spoke to her or not.

Mr Knightley stayed on at Hartfield when the others had all gone home.

'A strange game was played here tonight,' he said to Emma. 'I was watching Jane Fairfax and Frank Churchill. There is a secret between them, I am sure. I think that they are more than friends.'

Emma laughed and shook her head. 'A match between Jane Fairfax and Frank Churchill? No, you are wrong, very wrong, Mr Knightley,' Emma said. 'I do not think that Jane likes Frank at all. And I am sure that he does not admire her!'

Mr Knightley was not pleased by Emma's words and he left Hartfield soon afterwards.

12

Box Hill

It was now the middle of June and the weather was sunny and hot.

Mrs Elton was making plans for a picnic[73] on Box Hill. Box Hill was the most beautiful place in the neighbourhood. Mrs Elton and her friends were going to drive there in their carriages. They would take food and drink with them. Mrs Elton started to make all the arrangements!

Emma had never been to Box Hill and she wanted to go there. But she did not want to go with Mrs Elton.

Mr Knightley saw that the letters made the name, DIXON.

Mrs Elton went on with her plans for the picnic and then one of the horses went lame[74]. The visit to Box Hill could not take place that day.

'What shall we do, Knightley?' Mrs Elton cried. 'The weather is good now, but it may not be so good in a few days. And without the horses, we can go nowhere today.'

'You can come to Donwell Abbey,' Mr Knightley said. 'You will not need horses and carriages. You can walk from the village to my house. My strawberries[75] are very fine this year. Come to Donwell Abbey and eat them.'

Mrs Elton was delighted. 'What a good idea, Knightley,' she said. 'All our friends will be there, of course. I shall arrange everything for you. I arrange parties very well.'

'You may arrange parties in your own house, Mrs Elton, but not in mine,' Mr Knightley said. 'If I ever marry, my wife will make all the arrangements. Until then, I shall arrange things at Donwell Abbey myself.'

'Well, you are a strange man!' Mrs Elton said with a laugh. 'But I expect that my ideas will be the same as yours. Everything will be very easy, of course. We can all walk about, eat the strawberries and sit together for a picnic under the trees ...'

'I am sorry, but my ideas are different from yours, Mrs Elton,' Mr Knightley said. 'Eat strawberries in the garden, if you wish. But my servants will prepare food and we will eat it inside – in the dining-room. I want everyone to be cool and comfortable when they visit Donwell Abbey.'

Mr Knightley was thinking of Mr Woodhouse. He wanted the old man to enjoy a day at Donwell Abbey with his friends. If Mr Woodhouse had to sit outside on the grass and eat a meal, he would be upset. However, he *would* enjoy a meal while he sat in his good friend's dining-room.

Everyone accepted Mr Knightley's invitation to enjoy his delicious strawberries at Donwell Abbey. If the weather was fine on the following day, other horses could be found and everyone would drive to Box Hill.

Emma had not been to Donwell Abbey for a long time. First, she found a comfortable chair for her father in the library. Mr Knightley had put some interesting books and pictures on a table there. He knew that Mr Woodhouse would enjoy sitting quietly and looking at them. Then Emma went outside. She walked around the beautiful gardens and looked at the fine old house.

Everyone ate strawberries and praised the delicious fruit. But the sun was very hot and soon everyone went to sit in the cool shade under some trees. They were all happy, except for Mrs Weston. Frank had not arrived and she was worried about him. He was going to ride his horse to Donwell Abbey. She was worried that his horse had gone lame.

Mrs Elton was talking so loudly to Jane Fairfax that Emma could hear every word.

'It is time for you to make a decision, Miss Fairfax,' Mrs Elton was saying. 'It is now the middle of June. You cannot wait any longer. All the best positions for governesses will soon be taken. You must write a letter to my friend, Mrs Smallridge, tomorrow.'

Jane did not answer. She stood up and spoke to Mr Knightley.

'Would you like to take your guests around the Abbey gardens?' she asked with a smile. 'Everything is looking so beautiful.'

Mr Knightley was happy to do this and he led the way. His guests followed him and admired the gardens full of beautiful summer flowers. It was now extremely hot. Most people soon went to sit in the cool shade under the trees once again.

Beyond the trees, green fields went down to Abbey-Mill Farm. A river ran from the hills and down past the farm. It was a beautiful view.

Emma was surprised to see that Mr Knightley was walking with Harriet. He was having a pleasant conversation with her.

Very soon, it was time for everyone to go into the house and eat the delicious cold food that was ready for them.

After the meal, Emma stayed in the house to talk to her father and the rest of the party went out into the gardens again.

The heat of the day made Mr Woodhouse tired and he fell asleep in his chair. Emma walked into the hall. She looked out of the tall windows at the fine gardens. Suddenly she saw Jane Fairfax hurrying back into the house. The young woman looked hot and tired.

'Oh, Miss Woodhouse,' Jane said, 'I was looking for you. I am going home at once. I cannot find my aunt anywhere. Please will you tell her that I have gone – if you see her?'

'Of course I will,' Emma said. 'But surely you are not going to walk back to Highbury alone? Let me ask Mr Knightley if you can use his carriage.'

'Thank you, Miss Woodhouse, thank you very much. But I do not need a carriage. I walk fast. It will only take me twenty minutes,' Jane replied.

'But it is hot and you look tired,' Emma said kindly.

'I am tired – but only in my mind,' Jane replied. 'I want to walk and I need to be alone.' And she hurried away.

Emma returned to the library but her father was still asleep.

About fifteen minutes later, Frank Churchill came into the room. He looked hot and angry.

'I could not come before,' Frank said to Emma. 'Mrs Churchill is ill again. I shall have to go back to Richmond almost at once. I only came here because I made a promise. Where is everyone? I suppose that I am too late. People will be going home soon.

'I met one of the guests as I came to the house – Miss Fairfax,' Frank added. 'Why was she walking home now? It is madness to walk in this heat!'

Emma saw that Frank was not as cheerful as usual. The heat had made him bad tempered. At first, the young man refused to eat or drink, but after a time he went to find some cold beer. When he returned some time later, he was no longer bad tempered. But he did not look happy.

'I hope that you found something to eat and drink,' Emma said with a smile.

'Yes, thank you, Miss Woodhouse,' Frank replied. 'I am cooler now and feel much better. But I am not happy. I am not happy at all. My life has become very difficult. I am tired of doing nothing in Richmond. I can never be happy in England. I am sure of that. I think that I shall go overseas for a couple of years.'

'But you are happier now than when you first arrived at Donwell Abbey,' Emma said, smiling. 'We are all going to Box Hill tomorrow. It is a beautiful place. You must come with us, Mr Churchill. Your father and Mrs Weston have arranged everything.'

At first, Frank refused, but then he said, 'Well, if you wish me to stay in Highbury and go with you to Box Hill tomorrow, Miss Woodhouse, I will.'

———

Next day the weather was fine, and everyone got ready for the visit to Box Hill. Mr and Mrs Weston had made all the arrangements and everything was well planned. Everyone except Mrs Weston made the seven-mile journey to Box Hill in their carriages. Mrs Weston was expecting a child[76] and on this day she felt tired. She agreed to stay at Hartfield with Mr Woodhouse.

The countryside around them was beautiful, but no one seemed happy. The weather was very hot and the visitors were soon tired. They did not want to walk very far. Mr and Mrs Elton walked away by themselves. They did not talk to anyone. Things were a little better when everyone sat down on the grass to eat the picnic. Mr Weston had brought lots of delicious cold food and drink for everyone.

Frank Churchill sat next to Emma and began to pay her a lot of attention. His conversation was lively and interesting. Emma laughed at his words, but she did not really feel happy. Emma was not sure if Frank was happy or not.

'You are the one who is talking, Mr Churchill,' Emma said at last. 'Everyone else is silent. Why is that? What is everyone thinking about?'

Frank suddenly stood up. 'Why is everyone so quiet?' he said loudly. 'We have all come here to enjoy ourselves. But no one looks happy. Why not? Ladies and gentlemen, you heard Miss Woodhouse. She wants to know what each of you are thinking!'

Some people laughed, but the Eltons looked angry.

'Mr Churchill is not telling the truth,' Emma said with a laugh. 'I do not want to know what everyone is thinking. I cannot ask that.'

'Well, then, I have a better idea,' Frank said. 'There are eight of us here. This is what you must do. It is Miss Woodhouse's wish – everyone must say one very clever thing, or two things that are quite clever, or three things that are very dull.'

'Oh, that will be easy for me,' Miss Bates said happily. 'Three dull things. Yes. I shall be able to think of three dull things very easily!'

'*Only* three things, Miss Bates? That might be a problem,' Emma said. 'You will find it difficult to say *only* three dull things at one time, I am sure.'

At first, Miss Bates did not understand Emma's words. Then she blushed.

'I am not clever like my friend Miss Woodhouse,' she said. 'I talk too much and I do not think enough. I am sorry. I shall try to be quiet.'

'Only *three* things, Miss Bates? You will find it difficult to say
only *three dull things, I am sure.'*

There was silence and then Mrs Elton spoke.

'Miss Woodhouse, you will excuse Mr Elton and myself. We have nothing clever to say to you. We have nothing to say to you at all!'

The Eltons both stood up and began to walk away.

'They are a very good match,' Frank Churchill said to Emma. 'The Eltons knew each other for only a few weeks before they were married. Many men make mistakes when they choose their wives. Mr Elton was lucky. He chose a very suitable wife for himself.'

'Excuse me,' Jane Fairfax said quietly. 'People may know each other for a long time, but they still make mistakes about each other. They choose the wrong friends.

'It may be difficult to end a foolish friendship,' she went on. 'But only very weak people cannot end a friendship that is foolish. It can be done. I know.'

'Then I must be a weak person,' Frank replied. 'I would like someone to choose my wife for me. Would you do that, Miss Woodhouse? I am in no hurry, but my wife must be lively. She must have a beautiful complexion and have hazel eyes. She must be as charming as yourself! I shall return for her in two years.'

Emma smiled.

'Frank could be talking about Harriet,' she thought. 'Except that he wants a wife with hazel eyes.'

Jane's pale face had become red and she looked upset.

'Let us go for a walk, ma'am[77],' Jane said to her aunt.

Miss Bates and Jane Fairfax walked away and Mr Knightley followed them.

Frank Churchill went on talking and making jokes until even Emma was tired of him. She was very pleased when the servants said that the carriages were ready to leave.

Soon everyone began to walk slowly towards their own carriage.

The visit to Box Hill had not been pleasant for anyone. Everyone was glad to go home.

Mr Knightley walked up to Emma and spoke to her quietly.

'Emma, you have behaved very badly,' he said. 'You have been very rude to Miss Bates! And you were rude to her in front of all her friends! I could not believe that you made those remarks.'

Emma blushed and she tried to laugh.

'My remarks were not so very bad,' she said. 'I do not think that Miss Bates understood me.'

'Yes, she did understand you. Miss Bates understood you very well. But she did not make a remark about your bad behaviour herself. She is too kind.'

'Oh, Miss Bates is a good woman,' Emma said. 'Everyone knows that. But she is silly too, you must agree.'

'Perhaps she is silly,' Mr Knightley replied. 'Miss Bates is also old and very poor. She needs kindness from you, Emma, not rudeness. You are an important person in Highbury, and you should have behaved better. I am ashamed[78] of you.'

Mr Knightley helped Emma into her carriage. He did not say another word.

Emma was very unhappy and she could not speak.

She looked up once and held out her hand. But Mr Knightley had turned away and the carriage moved on.

Emma cried all the way home.

13

Secrets and Surprises

Early the next morning, Emma went to call on the Bateses.
Old Mrs Bates, who was alone in the small sitting-room,
smiled when she saw Emma.

'I am afraid that Jane is not very well,' Mrs Bates said.
'She has a very bad headache. My daughter is looking after
her.'

A few minutes later, Miss Bates came into the room. She
looked unhappy.

'I hear that Jane is not well,' Emma said. 'I am sorry.'

'Oh, Miss Woodhouse, you are so kind,' said Miss Bates. 'I
suppose that you have heard our news. I should be pleased,
but I am not. Poor Jane has been with us for such a long
time. Mother and I will miss her so much! Jane has been
writing letters to the Campbells and Mrs Dixon. She had
told them the news of her — you know — her new position.
She will be a governess. But she has been crying — and now
she has a bad headache. She really cannot see you ...'

'I am surprised that Miss Fairfax has accepted a position so
soon,' Emma said. 'I thought that she was waiting until
Colonel Campbell and the Dixons returned from Ireland.
Where is the position, Miss Bates? I hope that it is a good
one.'

'Oh, Miss Woodhouse — you are always so kind,' Miss
Bates replied. 'Jane is going to be a governess for Mrs
Smallridge. Her home is near Bristol. Jane will be looking
after three little girls —'

'And ... and Mrs Smallridge is a friend of Mrs Elton's?'
Emma said.

'Yes, she is. Mrs Smallridge wanted Jane to go to Bristol

three weeks ago. At first Jane said that she could not go so soon,' Miss Bates replied. 'We spent yesterday evening at Mrs Elton's house. Just before tea, we heard that Mr Frank Churchill had been called back to Richmond. Then after tea, poor dear Jane decided that she would go to Mrs Smallridge at once. The news was quite a surprise to me — quite a surprise! Oh, I see that you are looking at the piano, dear Miss Woodhouse. Well, it must stay there until Colonel Campbell comes back to England. It was his gift, or his daughter's perhaps — I do not know. Poor Jane. She is so upset. Please excuse me, Miss Woodhouse. I must go back to her. I will give Jane your good wishes.'

When Emma got back to Hartfield, Mr Knightley and Harriet were sitting with her father.

Mr Knightley stood up as Emma came into the room.

'I am going to London, Emma,' he said. 'I have come to say goodbye before I go.'

'Emma has been calling on our dear friend Miss Bates,' Mr Woodhouse said. 'She went there after breakfast, as I told you.'

Emma looked up at Mr Knightley and smiled at him. He understood why Emma had gone to the Bateses' house. He was pleased. Emma had made a bad mistake at Box Hill. But today she had behaved well and had shown good manners. Mr Knightley took Emma's hand, held it, and smiled too. In another minute, he had gone.

Emma told her father what Jane had decided. Mr Woodhouse was surprised and upset. He was very fond of Jane Fairfax. Emma and her father talked about the news all evening.

But the next day brought even more surprising news. Mrs Churchill was dead! No one had believed that the selfish old woman was ill. For the first time in twenty-five years, people found good things to say about her. Even Mr Weston was sorry, but he was also thinking about his son. Mrs Churchill's funeral[79] was going to take place in Yorkshire.

Emma thought about Frank too.

'Frank can make his own decisions about his future life now,' she said to herself. 'If he wanted to marry Harriet it would not be a problem now.'

Then Emma remembered that Jane Fairfax would soon be leaving Highbury. Emma was sorry that they had not been good friends and she invited Jane to spend a day at Hartfield. But Jane was ill. She was too ill to visit or even to write. She had bad headaches and could not eat.

Doctor Perry was very worried about Jane. He said that Jane was too ill to leave Highbury. He wanted her to rest. The doctor told Miss Bates that Jane's health would be in danger if she went to work for Mrs Smallridge.

Emma wrote to Jane again. She offered Jane a ride in the Woodhouses' carriage. Jane sent an answer to Hartfield. She was too ill to go out and she refused Emma's offer. But later that day, someone saw Jane walking in the fields near Highbury.

Then Emma understood that Jane did not want to see her and she was sorry.

———

About ten days after Mrs Churchill's death, Mr Weston called at Hartfield to see Emma.

'Please come to Randalls as soon as you can, Emma,' he said. 'Mrs Weston has something very important to tell you.' Emma was worried. 'Mr Weston, why cannot you tell me now?' she asked.

'No, I promised Mrs Weston that I would not tell you,' Mr Weston replied. 'Come back to Randalls with me now. But do not say anything that will worry your father.'

Emma told Mr Woodhouse that she was going for a walk and she hurried out with Mr Weston.

'Have you heard from Frank?' Emma asked as they walked away from Hartfield.

'Frank was at Randalls this morning, but he has gone again,' Mr Weston replied.

Emma was very surprised, but Mr Weston said nothing more.

They were soon at Randalls. Mr Weston left Emma with Mrs Weston, who was looking ill and unhappy.

'What is the trouble, my dear friend?' Emma asked her quickly. 'Please tell me at once. Has your news anything to do with Mr Frank Churchill?'

'Yes, it has,' Mrs Weston replied. 'Frank spoke to his father about an – an attachment[80], this morning. Frank is ... Frank is engaged to a young lady. He has promised to marry her.'

Emma was silent.

'Oh, Emma!' Mrs Weston cried, 'Frank Churchill and Miss Fairfax are *engaged to be married*! I cannot believe it. They have been engaged for eight months. They met in Weymouth and they have been engaged since October! They have kept their engagement a secret from everyone.'

Emma did not know what to say.

'I cannot believe it either. It is very strange,' she said.

'Mr Weston and I are both very upset,' Mrs Weston went on. 'We think that Frank has behaved very badly.' She smiled sadly and held Emma's hand.

'I understand why you spoke to me alone here,' Emma said quietly. 'But do not worry about me. I do not love Mr Frank Churchill. I used to have feelings for him. But he has been no more than a friend for the last two months.'

Mrs Weston looked a little happier. 'I am very pleased to hear that, my dear Emma. I am very pleased,' she said. 'At one time, our dearest wish was that you and Frank would love each other. But he was in love with Jane when he came to Highbury.'

'Frank may love Jane, but he has behaved very badly.' Emma said. 'Frank was not honest with me and he was not honest with Jane either.'

'Jane watched how Frank behaved in Highbury,' Mrs Weston said. 'She was sad and upset that their engagement was a secret. They quarrelled. Jane accepted the position with Mrs Smallridge and she did not tell Frank. As soon as Frank heard of Jane's plan to be a governess, he told his uncle, Mr Churchill, about the engagement. Then Frank rode back to Highbury and found that poor Jane was very ill. They both knew that there must be no more secrets. After that, Frank rode on to Randalls and told us everything.'

'Frank Churchill is a very lucky man,' Emma said with a smile. 'Because Jane Fairfax loves Frank Churchill, she did not tell her friends the truth about her relationship with him. Frank asked her not to speak about it and she has been true to[81] him. Her character is very good and I wish her every happiness.'

Mr Weston heard these words as he came into the room. He smiled as he held Emma's hand in his own.

'I congratulate you, Mr Weston,' Emma said, giving him her best wishes. 'You will soon have a daughter-in-law who is one of the best and one of the most beautiful young ladies in England!'

When she was back at Hartfield, Emma began to think about Harriet. Poor Harriet! She must now be told of Frank Churchill's engagement to Jane Fairfax.

'And I shall have to tell Harriet the news myself,' Emma thought. 'I have been very wrong. Because of me, Harriet believed that she could be Frank Churchill's wife. I gave her hope. I have been very foolish, very foolish indeed.'

Harriet came to Hartfield later that day. She ran into the sitting-room to speak to Emma.

'Have you heard the news, Miss Woodhouse?' she cried.

'What news?' Emma asked. But she knew what Harriet was going to say.

'The news about Jane Fairfax and Mr Frank Churchill, of course!' Harriet cried. 'They are to be married. Did you know that they were in love, Miss Woodhouse? I did not.'

'I did not know, Harriet. If I had known, I would have told you. I never wanted you to be unhappy,' Emma replied.

'I am not unhappy!' Harriet said with a laugh. 'Did you think that I wanted to be Mrs Frank Churchill? What a strange mistake! The man that I have feelings for is far, far better than Mr Churchill. This man is a true gentleman in every way!'

'Harriet,' Emma said carefully, 'we must understand each other. Are you speaking about Mr Knightley?'

'Of course,' Harriet replied. 'We have talked about him a lot. I thought that you understood what I was saying.'

'But Harriet,' said Emma. 'The gentleman whom you liked, helped you. That is what you said. It was Mr Frank Churchill who saved you from the gypsies. I thought that you were talking about him.'

Harriet laughed and shook her head.

'Mr Knightley danced with me at the ball, when I did not have a dancing-partner,' Harriet said. 'You remember that Mr Elton would not dance with me. Mr Knightley helped me that evening. He saved me. That was my meaning. Mr Knightley was very kind to me. He is the kindest man that I know. He is a gentleman in every way. I do hope that you will be happy for me, Miss Woodhouse – and for Mr Knightley too, of course.'

'Good God!' cried Emma. 'This is a terrible mistake. What can I do?'

'You do not have to do anything, Miss Woodhouse,' Harriet said with a happy smile.

'I know that Mr Knightley is a gentleman of society and

that I have no money. But if he does not care about that, why should I? I hope that you will be happy for us both.'

Emma was silent. Then she spoke, very quietly.

'Do you think that Mr Knightley feels the same way about you, Harriet?' Emma asked.

'Oh yes, Miss Woodhouse. I am pleased to say that I do think that,' Harriet replied.

Emma could not believe it. She tried to understand her own feelings. Why did the news about Harriet and Mr Knightley make her feel so unhappy? And then at last she knew the truth. Mr Knightley must marry Emma herself!

Emma had to listen to Harriet praising Mr Knightley and explaining her feelings for him.

'He was so kind to me at Donwell Abbey,' Harriet said. 'He paid a lot of attention to me. He walked with me and no one else. He asked me then if I had feelings for anyone. I did not answer, but I understood him at once.'

'Perhaps Mr Knightley was talking about Mr Martin,' Emma said.

'Oh no, Miss Woodhouse,' Harriet replied. 'Mr Knightley said nothing about Mr Martin. You taught me not to care for Mr Martin. No. Mr Knightley was talking about himself. I know that he has feelings for me. I am very happy.'

At that moment, Emma and Harriet heard Mr Woodhouse coming towards them.

'I must go, Miss Woodhouse,' Harriet said quickly. 'I shall tell your father my news some other time.'

Emma was very pleased that Harriet had left her alone. A few seconds later, she ran quickly upstairs to her own room.

'Oh God! I wish that I had never met Harriet Smith!' Emma cried.

———

Emma tried to understand her own feelings. She knew that she was very unhappy. She had made herself unhappy.

'I know that he has feelings for me.'

She knew now that she had never loved Mr Frank Churchill. He had flattered her and made her laugh, but that was all. Mr Knightley had been Emma's friend all her life. He was a far better gentleman than any other man that she had ever known. All her life, Emma had respected Mr Knightley. Now she knew that she loved him too. But it was too late.

'And I have spoilt Harriet,' Emma said to herself. 'Harriet is a kind, simple girl. She could have been happy with Robert Martin. But I told her that she could marry a gentleman. I made Harriet think that Mr Elton was in love with her. I was wrong. I invited Harriet to Hartfield, where she saw Mr Knightley nearly every day. I praised her and flattered her. Harriet believes that a gentleman like Mr Knightley could love her because of me. How I wish that Harriet and Mr Knightley had never met! I shall never be happy again.'

14

More Than a Friend

Emma knew now that her own happiness depended on Mr Knightley and his feelings for her. Emma had no hope that Mr Knightley loved her. She could only hope for his respect.

Emma could not think of marriage herself, because she could never leave her father. But when she thought of Mr Knightley marrying Harriet, or anyone else, she became very unhappy. Mr Knightley was Emma's friend and he had always told her the truth. She could not think of her life without his friendship and advice.

Mr Knightley was still in London, but he would soon be home. Emma would then have to see Mr Knightley and Harriet together. Until then, she did not wish to see Harriet at all.

Emma wrote to her friend and asked her to stay away from Hartfield for a time.

Mrs Weston was the next visitor to Hartfield and she had more to tell Emma about Frank Churchill and Jane Fairfax. For a few hours, Mrs Weston's interesting story stopped Emma thinking about Harriet and Mr Knightley.

Mrs Weston had been to see Jane Fairfax and she had invited Jane out for a drive in the Westons' carriage. At first, Jane had refused, but then she had agreed to go with Mrs Weston. The two ladies had had a long conversation.

'Jane has not had a happy moment since she agreed to the secret engagement. This is what she told me,' Mrs Weston said. 'She knew that the secret engagement was wrong. But her love for Frank was the first thing in her mind. She depended on Frank for her future happiness.

'Jane and Frank had quarrelled about their engagement several times,' Mrs Weston went on. 'Jane knew that it was wrong to keep it a secret. But Frank refused to agree with her. He knew that the engagement would have made Mrs Churchill very angry. Frank wanted to be happy – and he was at first. He could not understand Jane's feelings.

'But Jane is happy now, Emma,' Mrs Weston went on. 'She thanks you for your kindness to her.'

'I have not been kind enough,' Emma said. 'I could have been a better friend to Jane Fairfax.'

———

Emma now had the rest of the day to think about her own mistakes. It was July, but the weather was cold and wet. Emma could not go out and the bad weather made Mr Woodhouse feel ill. It was an unhappy day at Hartfield.

Emma now believed that she would never have happiness in the future. Only other people would be happy. When Mrs Weston's baby was born, she would have less time to spend with Emma. Frank Churchill and Jane would be married and they would go to live in Yorkshire. Mr Knightley would be happy with Harriet and he would have no reason to visit Hartfield every day.

Emma would have plenty of time to understand her own feelings and become a better person.

The next morning, the bad weather continued, but in the afternoon the sun shone. Emma decided to go for a walk. She was in the garden when she saw Mr Knightley walking towards her. He smiled and they walked along together. Mr Knightley said nothing. Emma felt that she had to speak.

'I have some news to tell you,' she said. 'It will surprise you.'

'What is your news?' Mr Knightley asked.

'The very best kind – news of a wedding!' Emma replied.

'If you are talking about Miss Fairfax and Frank Churchill, I know already,' Mr Knightley said. 'Mr Weston wrote to me this morning and told me everything. The news was not a surprise to me.'

'It may not have been a surprise to you, but it was to me,' Emma said quietly. 'I could not believe it. I have been very silly. I have not understood anything.'

Mr Knightley stopped walking and looked at Emma kindly.

'You are sad now,' he said. 'Frank Churchill has behaved very badly to you, Emma. But he will soon be far away from Highbury. You will be able to forget him one day. I feel sorry for Jane Fairfax. She should have someone better than Frank Churchill.'

'Mr Knightley,' Emma replied. 'You are wrong about me. I have never loved Frank Churchill. He flattered me and paid a lot of attention to me. But that was to hide his secret love for Jane. I did not understand that. I have been very silly and

I hope that they will both be very happy together.'

'I have never liked Frank Churchill, but he is a very lucky man,' Mr Knightley said. 'He has behaved very badly and everyone loves him. He is loved by a beautiful young woman who is both clever and good. He made her unhappy but she was true to him. His aunt died and he is no longer dependent on her for his future happiness. He now has money and he is free. He can marry whoever he wants. And he is still young – only twenty-three! He will have a happy future. Frank Churchill is a *very* lucky young man.'

'You do not sound happy, Mr Knightley,' Emma said. 'Do you envy[82] Frank Churchill?'

'There is one thing that makes me envy him,' Mr Knightley said.

Emma did not answer.

'Perhaps you do not want to know why I envy Frank Churchill,' Mr Knightley went on. 'But I must tell you!'

'Do not say anything that will make you unhappy!' Emma cried.

'Well, then, I shall be silent,' Mr Knightley replied. Emma saw that he was very upset.

'You can speak to me as a friend, Mr Knightley,' Emma said quietly. 'Tell me what you want to say.'

'Then I will speak, but not just as a friend,' Mr Knightley replied. 'My dear Emma, have I any hope of being more than a friend to you?'

Emma could not answer.

'Your silence does give me hope,' Mr Knightley said. 'But my dearest, dearest Emma, please tell me now – at once. You might say no, but I must hear your answer!'

Emma was too happy to speak.

'If I loved you less, I could talk about it more,' Mr Knightley said. 'I am not a clever talker like Frank Churchill. But I have always told you the truth and I am telling you the truth now. It

'If I loved you less, I could talk about it more.'

is time for you to tell me what you think, dearest Emma.'

Then Emma found the right words to say and she said them.

In the next half hour, Emma and Mr Knightley talked about everything. They talked about mistakes and quarrels and love. When Emma and Mr Knightley returned to the house together their happiness was perfect.

Mr Woodhouse was glad to see Mr Knightley again. He asked him all about his visit to London. Mr Woodhouse did not know that his good friend was planning to marry his daughter and take her away from him!

Emma did not sleep well that night. She was very happy, but there were two people who would not like her news – her father and Harriet. How could Emma tell her father about her engagement? And how could she tell Harriet?

Emma and Mr Knightley could become engaged but Emma knew that she could never leave her father. While Mr Woodhouse was alive, she could never marry and leave Hartfield.

Harriet Smith was a different problem. In the morning, Emma wrote her young friend a letter. She told Harriet what had happened. A servant took the letter to Mrs Goddard's school.

Emma also wrote a letter to her sister Isabella. Emma asked Isabella to invite Harriet to stay with her. It would be better for Harriet to leave Highbury. If Harriet lived in London for a few weeks, she would forget her love for Mr Knightley more quickly.

Mr Knightley came to Hartfield for breakfast. He saw that Emma was sad from writing the letters. But before he left, she was happy again.

At midday, a parcel arrived from Randalls. Inside this parcel there was a short letter from Mrs Weston, and a very long letter from Frank Churchill to the Westons.

Mrs Weston's note said:

Mr Weston and I would like you to read Frank's letter. We have forgiven him. We want our friends to understand him and to forgive him too.

Emma read Frank's letter quickly.

She knew most of the story already, from Mrs Weston. But towards the end of the letter she learnt something new.

I behaved very badly at Box Hill, Frank had written. *I talked to no one but Miss Woodhouse. I wanted to make Jane jealous. I thought that Miss Woodhouse had guessed the truth about Jane and myself. And I thought that she would understand.*

Jane was cold to me that day because I behaved badly. I made her very unhappy. And I did not talk to her again that day, because I left for Richmond.

After the visit to Box Hill, Jane wrote me a letter. She told me that she was ending our engagement. Her letter arrived on the day that Mrs Churchill died. Of course, I answered Jane's letter at once. But I had to make many arrangements after Mrs Churchill's death. I am afraid that my letter to Jane was not sent.

A few days later, when Jane had not received a reply from me, she wrote to me again. She returned all my letters. She also asked me to return all the letters that she had written to me.

I told my uncle everything and hurried back to Highbury. Thank God, I was not too late. My dearest Jane is now dearer to me than ever. I know that Jane is a much better person than I am. I cannot believe that she loves me. I am a very lucky man.

Your loving son,

F.C. Weston Churchill

When Mr Knightley next came to Hartfield, Emma showed him the letter and asked him to read it.

'I would rather talk to you, Emma, but I will read it,' he said. 'What a long letter that young man has written!'

Mr Knightley read the letter quickly and was specially interested in the parts about Emma herself.

'So, Frank Churchill spent all his time talking to you so that Jane would be jealous!' Mr Knightley said angrily. 'He thought that you had guessed his secret. And he thought that you would understand! All he ever thought about was himself.

'... And it was Frank Churchill who sent the piano to Jane Fairfax! I thought so,' said Mr Knightley. 'Only a very thoughtless young man would have sent a gift like that to Highbury.

'Well, this last page shows that Mr Churchill is very fond of Miss Fairfax,' Knightley said. 'Jane Fairfax is much too good for him, as he says. But he does seem to love her. I agree with him. He is a very lucky young man.'

Mr Knightley gave the letter back to Emma.

'Let us now talk about something else,' he said. 'I have had enough of Frank Churchill for one day.'

Mr Knightley took Emma's hand and held it in his own.

'Emma, I have been thinking about your father,' Mr Knightley said. 'I know what you want to tell me. You want to say that our marriage is impossible. It is impossible because it would make your father too unhappy. If you tell him that you want to leave Hartfield, he will never agree. He will not agree to live with us at Donwell Abbey either.

'So this is my plan. After our marriage, I shall live with you and your father here, at Hartfield. What do you say to that, my dearest Emma?'

The more Emma thought about this plan, the better she liked it.

Her father must soon be told about their engagement, but not just yet!

15

Future Happiness

Harriet answered Emma's letter politely, but she did not wish to meet her. Isabella had invited Harriet to stay with her family in London for two weeks. Harriet accepted the invitation and soon she travelled to London. Mr Knightley came to Hartfield every day and Emma was now very, very happy.

Emma went to call on Jane Fairfax, who was still living with her aunt and grandmother. This time, Jane ran down the stairs and greeted Emma warmly. Jane looked very happy and beautiful.

Emma was about to speak when she heard Mrs Elton's voice in the little sitting-room. So Emma just smiled and held Jane's hand for a moment. Then both young women walked upstairs.

Miss Bates was not at home, so Mrs Elton was sitting and talking to old Mrs Bates. Mrs Elton was looking very cheerful and Emma soon knew why. Mrs Elton knew about Jane's secret engagement and she thought that Emma did not know about it.

'Well, Miss Woodhouse, do you not think that our dear friend, Jane, is looking much better?' Mrs Elton said with a laugh. 'Dr Perry must be a very fine doctor. But perhaps he has had help from a certain young man ... no, no. I promised that I would not say anything. We must all visit Box Hill again soon, Miss Woodhouse. Some of us were not feeling very happy that afternoon!'

Soon after this, Miss Bates returned to the house.

'Oh, my dear Miss Woodhouse! I am delighted that you have come! Yes, our dear Jane is now — so much better. Dr

Perry — such a charming young man. And Mrs Elton! You are here too — bringing Jane good wishes for — for — Oh! Mr Elton will be coming here soon? I —'

Miss Bates sounded even more worried and nervous than usual.

Mrs Elton smiled and nodded. 'Mr Elton is meeting me here. He is very late,' she said. 'Mr Knightley must be busy with him at Donwell Abbey. Mr Elton was meeting him there, you know.'

When Mr Elton arrived, he was hot and tired.

'Knightley was not at Donwell Abbey,' he said angrily. 'I walked all that way and in the heat – for nothing. Knightley's servants did not know where he was. Knightley does not usually forget meetings of that kind.'

Emma smiled. She guessed that Mr Knightley was at Hartfield, waiting to see her. She stood up and Jane walked downstairs with her.

'I very much wanted to talk to you, Miss Woodhouse,' she said. 'But with Mrs Elton there ...'

'... I might have asked too many questions,' Emma said, finishing Jane's sentence. She smiled. 'You must be tired of answering them.'

'I am happy that you are so interested in me, after all that has happened,' Jane replied. 'I should be giving you apologies and reasons for my bad behaviour. I was so cold to you but I could not explain why. The secret was not only mine, as you know.'

'Say no more,' Emma said. 'Let us forgive each other at once. You will soon be leaving Highbury and all your friends here.'

'I shall stay in Highbury until the Campbells and the Dixons return from Ireland,' Jane replied. 'There will be three months of mourning[83] for Mrs Churchill and then Frank and I will be married.'

'I am so pleased that you are not leaving Highbury yet,' Emma said. 'I am so pleased that you and Mr Churchill will be together. And I am pleased that we will be friends!'

———

A few days later, Mrs Weston gave birth to her baby. The Westons named the little girl Anna. All the Westons' friends were delighted.

'I am sure that little Anna Weston will be as spoilt as you were, Emma,' Mr Knightley said with a laugh. 'But spoilt children improve as they get older. You were spoilt and you improved, my dearest Emma.' Then he stopped laughing and looked into her beautiful hazel eyes. 'You have called me Mr Knightley since you were a child. From today, I should like you to call me by my first name – George.'

'Oh, I cannot do that!' replied Emma, smiling. 'I have always called you Mr Knightley and I shall continue to call you Mr Knightley. I shall call you George just once – in church, when we are married.'

Mr Knightley showed Emma a letter from his brother John. In his letter, John congratulated them both on their engagement. The family would be coming to Hartfield in August, and Harriet would return to Highbury with them.

Emma now knew that she must tell her father about her engagement to Mr Knightley. She made her plan carefully. First Emma would tell her father the news and then Mr Knightley would come in and speak to Mr Woodhouse too.

At first, when he heard the news, old Mr Woodhouse was very upset. He could not understand why Emma wanted to get married.

'You and I are happy are we not, Emma?' he said. 'Mr Knightley comes to Hartfield nearly every day. Why must anything change? First Isabella got married. Then dear Miss Taylor got married and now you. This news is very upsetting.'

'But Isabella and Miss Taylor both *left* Hartfield, Papa,'

Emma said. 'Mr Knightley will be living *here* with us. He will look after us both.'

After thinking for several minutes, Mr Woodhouse agreed to the arrangement.

Next, the Westons had to be told the good news. They were surprised, but very happy. Mr Weston had soon told everyone in Highbury.

Everyone in Highbury approved of the match – except for the Eltons. Mr Elton did not care very much. But Mrs Elton did not like the news at all. Emma Woodhouse was going to become Mrs George Knightley! Mrs Elton was not pleased.

'Poor Knightley,' Mrs Elton said to her husband. 'And how clever of Miss Woodhouse to have caught the most important gentleman in Highbury. It is a pity that we can never invite Knightley to the vicarage alone again!'

———

Time passed quickly and it was nearly August.

Mr Knightley came to Hartfield one day and said, 'I have something to tell you, Emma. I do not know if you will think that my news is good or bad.'

'You are smiling, so it must be good news,' Emma replied. 'If you are happy, then I am happy too. Who or what is the news about?'

'Harriet Smith,' Mr Knightley replied. 'Harriet Smith is to marry Robert Martin.'

At first, Emma was so surprised that she could not speak.

'You are not happy about it, Emma,' Mr Knightley said.

'No – no, you are wrong,' Emma replied. 'I am very happy. But I cannot believe that Robert Martin has proposed to Harriet again and that she has accepted him. Tell me more. How, where, when did this happen?'

'Robert Martin went to London on business three days ago,' Mr Knightley said. 'I asked him to take some papers to my brother John. That evening, John and his family invited

Robert Martin to the theatre and Harriet Smith was there too. They all had a good time. The next day, John invited Robert to dine with them. After dinner, Robert spoke to Harriet. He proposed to her again and his proposal was accepted.

'I saw Robert this morning,' Mr Knightley went on, 'and he was very happy. I am sure that Harriet will soon tell you more.'

Emma was so happy that she wanted to dance and sing. After five unhappy weeks, Harriet had found happiness again.

The next day, Mr Woodhouse and Emma went to Randalls to see the Westons and their new baby. They were sitting with Mrs Weston, when two people walked past the window.

'It is Frank and Miss Fairfax,' Mrs Weston said. 'Frank came here this morning and Miss Fairfax is spending the day with us too.'

A few minutes later, Jane, Frank and Mr Weston came into the sitting-room. Mr Weston was carrying his baby daughter. Everyone admired the beautiful child.

Frank walked over to Emma and sat next to her.

'I must thank you, Miss Woodhouse,' the young man said quietly. 'You wrote kind words about me in your letter to Mrs Weston. I hope that you have not changed your mind about me!'

'No, Mr Churchill. I am pleased to see you again and to shake your hand,' Emma said.

Frank smiled and looked at Jane.

'She is looking well, is she not?' he said. 'Miss Woodhouse, I am surprised that you did not guess our secret. I nearly told you once. I should have told you. I know that now.

'I hope that my uncle, Mr Churchill, will come from Richmond to see Jane soon,' Frank said. 'I feel so far away from her when I cannot be in Highbury. Are you not sorry for me, Miss Woodhouse?'

'I am *very sorry* for you, Mr Churchill,' Emma said with a laugh.

Frank smiled. 'I have to give you and Mr Knightley my congratulations too,' Frank said. 'Mr Knightley is a very fine, good gentleman. But do look at Jane, Miss Woodhouse. Is she not beautiful, with her pale skin and dark hair? She is far too good for me!'

When Emma left Randalls, she thought about Frank Churchill and Mr Knightley. Emma knew that Mr Knightley was a much finer gentleman than Frank Churchill.

A few days later, John Knightley brought his family to Highbury and Harriet was with them.

Emma immediately gave Harriet her congratulations and the pretty girl looked very happy. Soon Robert Martin was invited to Hartfield too.

In the next few weeks, Harriet did not see so much of her dear friend Emma Woodhouse. Harriet was too busy at Abbey-Mill Farm, planning her wedding.

Before the end of September, Robert Martin and Harriet Smith were married. The vicar, Mr Elton, performed their marriage ceremony[84] in the little church in Highbury.

By that time, Jane Fairfax had left Highbury and she was living in London with the Campbells. Mr Frank Churchill was in London too. Jane and Frank were going to get married there in November.

Mr Knightley and Emma planned to get married in October, while John Knightley and his family were still in Highbury. But Mr Woodhouse was very unhappy when he heard the news. October was far too soon! Emma did not want to upset her father. She did not know what to do.

Then something happened which made Mr Woodhouse change his mind. Thieves stole some chickens from Mrs

Weston's poultry-house[85] one night. Chickens were stolen from other people's poultry-houses on following nights. Mr Woodhouse was very frightened and upset.

'The same thieves might break a window at Hartfield, climb inside the house, and steal everything,' he said. Then he thought about Mr Knightley.

'If Mr Knightley comes to live at Hartfield, we will all be safe,' he said happily.

So Mr Knightley and Emma suggested a day in October for their wedding and old Mr Woodhouse was happy to agree.

Only a few friends were invited to the quiet wedding and Mr Elton performed the ceremony.

Mrs Elton was not there, but she heard all about it from Mr Elton. He described the wedding ceremony and Miss Woodhouse's dress. Mrs Elton was very disappointed with her husband's description of the wedding.

'Your description makes me believe that the dress was not elegant and that the ceremony was very dull,' she said to her husband.

However, all the true friends of Emma Woodhouse and George Knightley thought differently. They thought that Emma's dress was very elegant, she looked very beautiful, and the ceremony was perfect. And all the friends' good wishes came true. The marriage of Mr and Mrs George Knightley was a long and very happy one.

The ceremony was perfect.

Points for Understanding

1

1 Describe these people. How are they related? (a) Emma
   Woodhouse (b) Mr Woodhouse (c) Isabella Knightley (d) George
   Knightley (e) John Knightley (f) Miss Taylor (g) Mr Weston
   (h) Frank Churchill
2 What are these things: (a) polite society (b) good manners?

2

Why does Mr Knightley quarrel with Emma?

3

1 Mr John Knightley likes to tease people. Who does he tease in this
   chapter? What does he say?
2 His words make everyone leave the party at Randalls. Why?
3 What happens next to Emma?

4

1 The name of Frank Churchill always makes Mr Knightley angry.
   What does Mr Knightley say about the young man?
2 Who lives in a very small house in the centre of Highbury and why
   does Emma feel that these people are dull?
3 Find twelve pieces of information about Jane Fairfax in this
   chapter.

5

Mr Knightley and Emma have different opinions about Jane Fairfax.
   What does each of them think about her and why?

6

1 Why does Emma change her mind and go to Mr and Mrs Coles' dinner party?
2 Who does Frank Churchill pay a lot of attention to?
3 Mrs Weston believes that Mr Knightley is in love with someone. Who? Why does she think this?

7

1 What 'brings back happy memories' to Frank Churchill?
2 Emma believes that Jane Fairfax is hiding a secret. What is it?
3 (a) What idea does Frank have? (b) Why is Mr Woodhouse upset about it? (c) Who has a better idea? (d) What stops these plans?
4 Why is Harriet very upset?

8

1 Emma thinks that someone is vulgar. Who? Why does she think this?
2 One day, Mrs Weston and Mr Knightley visit Hartfield. (a) Who does Emma tease Mr Knightley about? (b) What and who does he remind Emma about?

9

1 Why does Jane Fairfax walk in the rain?
2 Why are: (a) Mr Woodhouse (b) Mrs Elton, worried about Jane?

10

1 Why do you think that Frank was restless on the evening of the ball?
2 Who is rude to Harriet and who shows her kindness?
3 Why does Emma feel happy that evening?

11

This chapter could have been called 'Word Games'. Why?

12

Find examples of good manners and bad manners in this chapter.

13

1 Why do you think that Jane Fairfax has become ill?
2 What important things happen to: (a) Jane Fairfax (b) Frank Churchill (c) Harriet Smith (d) Emma Woodhouse, in this chapter?

14

In this chapter, whose future happiness depends on whom?

15

How do these people feel at the end of the story and why? (a) Miss Bates (b) The Westons (c) Robert Martin (d) Mrs Elton.

Glossary

1 **county** (page 4)
the United Kingdom of Great Britain is made up of England, Scotland, Wales and Northern Ireland. Each of these areas are divided into smaller areas called *counties*. See the map on page 7. The land outside towns, where there are farms, trees, mountains and lakes, is called the *countryside*. This word is often shortened to the *country*.

2 **clergyman** (page 4)
clergymen, or *vicars*, work in Christian churches and they lead the religious ceremonies. Vicars are leaders of the Protestant Christian religion. They live in houses called *vicarages*.

3 **parks** (page 4)
places in towns where people can sit, walk and play games. There are usually trees and gardens of flowers in *parks*. Sometimes there are lakes. In the nineteenth century, large houses in the country were often surrounded by parks. 'Park' is also sometimes used as the name of a house or property. For example: *Norland Park*.

4 **relatives** (page 4)
relatives are members of a family – particularly those members who do not live together.
A *niece* is the daughter of your brother or sister. A *nephew* is the son of your brother or sister. You are their *aunt* or *uncle*. See The People in This Story on pages 8 and 9.
An *in-law* is someone who you are related to by marriage. For example: Mr John Knightley is Emma Woodhouse's *brother-in-law*. Mr Woodhouse is Mr John Knightley's *father-in-law*. Mrs Campbell is Mr Dixon's *mother-in-law*. Mr John Knightley is Mr Woodhouse's *son-in-law*, etc.
When a man who has children marries again, his new wife becomes *stepmother* to his children. The man's children become his wife's *stepchildren*.

5 **changed her mind** – *to change her mind* (page 5)
decide to do something different, or to make a new plan. Jane first agreed to marry Mr Bigg-Wither, then she made a decision not to marry him. She *changed her mind*.

119

6 **inherited** – *to inherit* (page 5)

receive money or property from someone who has died. The money or property that a person receives is their *inheritance*. An *heir* is the person who will receive money or property when another person dies.

7 **visiting card** (page 5)

a small card with your name printed on it.

8 **suitable** (page 6)

in the nineteenth century, parents believed that it was important for their children to marry well. If their children's husbands or wives came from rich and powerful families, these were *suitable* marriages. A man and a woman who both came from good families, both had a good education, and both liked the same things were *suited* to each other.

Suitable books were well-written and they improved someone's knowledge and education when they read them.

9 **neighbourhood** (page 10)

a *neighbour* is a person who lives near you. The area around your home is the *neighbourhood*.

10 **Abbey** (page 10)

a large building next to a church where men or women live and pray to God. The word 'Abbey' is also sometimes used as the name of a property or a place because an abbey used to stand there. For example: *Abbey-Mill Farm* and *Donwell Abbey*.

11 **respected** – *to respect someone* (page 10)

when people think that someone is good, intelligent and behaves well, they *respect* that person.

12 **widower** (page 10)

a man whose wife has died.

13 **charming** (page 10)

pleasant and very attractive.

14 **governess** (page 11)

a *governess* was an unmarried woman who went to live in the house of another family. She looked after the children of the family and taught them. At the time of this story, women who had no money of their own had to find work. They usually tried to find a *position* – a job – as a governess.

15 **sighed** – *to sigh* (page 11)

the soft sound that someone makes because they are sad, tired or disappointed.

16 **Papa** (page 11)

the word that a son or a daughter uses for his or her father. *Grandmamma* is the word that a person uses for their grandmother.

17 **finding fault** – *to find fault with someone* (page 12)

when you do something which makes a problem for another person, it is *your fault* that they have the problem.

When you see that someone often does things wrong and you tell them about it each time, you are always *finding fault* with them.

18 **made the match** – *to make a match* (page 12)

Emma believed that Mr Weston and Miss Taylor were both kind, intelligent people who were interested in the same things. She thought that they were a *good match*. She arranged a meeting between them, hoping that they would fall in love and get married. Emma *made the match* between Mr Weston and Miss Taylor. She likes being a *matchmaker*. She is always *matchmaking* – looking for people who should marry each other.

19 **good company** (page 13)

if a person is *good company* they are lively and say interesting things. If you *enjoy a woman's company* you like being with her.

20 **gentleman** (page 13)

gentleman was the word used in the nineteenth century for a man from polite society.

A *real gentleman* was a man who had good manners. He was always polite and honest and he cared about other people's feelings.

21 **plump** (page 13)

not thin. A polite way of saying that someone is a little fat.

22 **admired** – *to admire* (page 13)

if you like the way that someone or something looks, or works, or behaves, you *admire* that person or thing.

23 **flatters** – *to flatter someone* (page 13)

a way of speaking to someone so that they like you and they do what you want. *Flattery* is telling someone that they are clever or attractive.

24 **praising** – *to praise* (page 14)

if you think that someone is clever, interesting or attractive and you tell another person this, you are *praising* the first person.

25 **hazel** (page 14)

light golden brown.

26 **complexion and figure** (page 14)

a person with a *good complexion* has smooth and attractive skin on their face.

121

Figure is the word used when you are describing a person's body. A person with a *good figure* has an attractive body which is a good shape.

27 **fond of** – *to be fond of someone* (page 14)
like and care for someone very much because you know them well.

28 **guardians** (page 16)
people who look after a child or a young person who has no mother or father.

29 **in trade** (page 16)
a merchant is a person who *trades* – buys and sells goods. Their business is *in trade*. At the time of this story, people who were in trade were usually at a lower level in polite society.

30 **shawl** (page 18)
a covering made of cloth or wool that a woman wears over her shoulders.

31 **catch a cold** – *to catch a cold* (page 18)
become ill after you have been wet and cold for too long. While you have a cold, you might have a *sore throat*. The inside of your throat is dry and painful.

32 **frame** (page 18)
the piece of wood or metal that is put around the edge of a painting so that it can be hung on a wall.

33 **equal** (page 21)
if a person's wealth, education and place in society is the same as your own, they are your *equal*.

34 **spoilt** – *to spoil* (page 21)
change someone in a bad way. When someone suddenly has rich friends, lots of expensive things and a comfortable home, they will not want to go back to their old life. Their new life has *spoilt* them. A rich, selfish person who does what they want and will not listen to advice is *spoilt*. Spoilt people believe that they can have whatever they want, whenever they want it.

35 **quarrel** – *to quarrel* (page 22)
argue with someone who you know well.

36 **bowing** – *to bow* (page 23)
bend your head and the top part of your body towards someone when you meet them. *Bowing* was the polite way that men greeted someone in the nineteenth century.

37 **bootlace** (page 23)
a strong thread that closes the front of a boot.

38 **housekeeper** (page 24)

a woman who looks after a house. It is the housekeeper's job to make sure that the house is clean and that meals are prepared.

39 **took no notice of it** – *to take no notice of something* (page 25)

Isabella knows that her husband is sometimes angry or rude. She does not say anything because she is not upset by his behaviour. She *takes no notice* when he is angry or rude.

40 **tease** – *to tease* (page 25)

say something to someone which makes them feel uncomfortable or angry. You *tease* someone because you want to have fun.

Mr John Knightley is not unkind when he teases people. However, *teasing* can sometimes be cruel or unkind.

41 **dine** – *to dine* (page 26)

eat a meal. When you invite friends to your house to eat a special meal in the evening, you are inviting them to a *dinner party*.

At the time of this story, dinner was eaten at about four o'clock in the afternoon.

42 **frowned** – *to frown* (page 29)

move your eyebrows down and closer together. People *frown* because they are angry, worried or are thinking carefully.

43 **blame** – *to blame someone* (page 32)

if you think that someone has made problems for you, or made you unhappy, you will *blame* that person for your problems and your unhappiness.

44 **duty** – *do his duty* (page 33)

Frank must do the best and most correct things to help his family.

45 **dependent** – *to be dependent* (page 33)

if you are *dependent* on someone, you need them because they give you money to live. You are their *dependant*.

An *independent* person makes decisions about their life. They also have strong feelings about the things that they like or dislike.

46 **dull** (page 34)

not interesting or exciting. Boring.

47 **deaf** (page 34)

not able to hear clearly.

48 **'It is a pity'** (page 34)

words that you say when you are disappointed about something.

49 **given us her opinion** – *to give an opinion* (page 36)

your *opinions* are your thoughts about someone or something.

If you have a *good opinion* of someone, you like them, and you think that they are a good person.

123

If, later, you do not have anything good to say about that person, or thing, you have *changed your opinion* of them.

50 **reserved** – *to be reserved* (page 45)
Jane Fairfax does not show her feelings. She is quiet and she thinks a lot. She is *reserved*.

51 **screen** (page 46)
a tall, flat piece of furniture which is used to separate one part of a room from another.
Screens also stop cold air – *draughts* – from making people feel uncomfortable. Note: draught is pronounced **draft**.

52 **paying ... a lot of attention** – *to pay a lot of attention to someone* (page 47)
spend a lot of time with someone and show that you are only interested in them and their thoughts and ideas.

53 **curls** (page 49)
pieces of hair that have curved or twisted shapes. See illustration on page 51.

54 **first dancing position** (page 50)
at the time of this story, people danced in groups. They did not dance alone. A man and a woman – a *couple* – danced together with other couples of dancers.
Each dancer stood in a line opposite their *dancing-partner*. As they danced, the couples moved up and down the room. They changed their *dancing positions*.

55 **ribbon** (page 52)
a thin piece of material which is used to tie things together. *Ribbons* are also sometimes used as decorations on clothes or hats. In the nineteenth century, many women had hats which they tied onto their heads with ribbons.
See the illustration on page 35.

56 **spectacles** (page 53)
eye glasses. Someone uses a *pair of spectacles* to help them to see more clearly.

57 **tunes** (page 53)
songs or pieces of music.

58 **happy memories** – *to bring back happy memories* (page 54)
the music that Frank is hearing makes him remember happy times that he spent with Jane.

59 **headache** (page 60)
a pain in your head.

60 **vulgar** (page 60)

Mrs Elton does not have a good education and she does not care about other people's feelings. Mrs Elton speaks and behaves in an impolite way. She is *vulgar*.

61 **vain** (page 61)

someone who thinks that they are good looking and important is *vain*.

62 **introductions** (page 61)

information about a person's family and where they live. At the time of this story, it was correct behaviour to be *introduced* to someone whom you did not know.

Introductions were either spoken or written in a letter. If someone was visiting a place for the first time, they asked a friend to tell everyone this information.

63 **Knightley** (page 62)

people from the same level in society sometimes called men by only their last names. They did not say the word 'Mr' before the man's last name. They would only do this if they knew the man well. Mrs Elton is not behaving correctly and she is showing bad manners. She is talking about Mr Knightley in a very informal way. She does not know him well and she is not from his level in society.

64 **a dress of lace and a long necklace of pearls** (page 66)

material with an attractive pattern which is formed from thin threads is called *lace*.

The valuable white stones which are sometimes found inside the bodies of some sea creatures are called *pearls*. Women often wore pearls on thin threads around their necks – *necklaces*.

65 **stockings** (page 68)

thin coverings that people wear on their legs.

66 **shy** (page 69)

quiet people who do not like talking to strangers are *shy*.

67 **umbrella** (page 72)

a thing that you hold over your head when it is raining.

68 **expect you to dance with her first** (page 73)

at this time, the man who arranged a ball and the most important woman from society danced together first.

A new wife was more important than other women. She was shown *respect* by the other women in her society. (See Glossary No. 11).

A new wife danced in the *first dancing position* in the first dance at a ball. (See Glossary No. 54) She also walked into a dining-room first, before everyone started their meal.

This was the custom. After several months passed, or until another woman got married, the woman at the highest level in society became the most important woman again.

69 **brother and sister** (page 77)
Knightley and Emma have been very good friends for many years. They know each other very well, almost like a brother and sister. In polite society, brothers and sisters never danced together.

70 **fainted** – *to faint* (page 77)
suddenly fall to the ground because you are ill or have had a shock. Someone who *faints* cannot see or hear for a short time.

71 **gypsies** (page 77)
people who do not live in houses, or stay in one place for very long. In the nineteenth century, *gypsies* travelled round the country in waggons pulled by horses. They lived in their waggons.

72 **piece of plaster** (page 79)
a strip of material which you stick onto your skin where there is a small cut, or a wound.

73 **picnic** (page 82)
a meal which is eaten outside when the weather is fine.

74 **went lame** – *to go lame* (page 84)
the horse has injured its foot or its leg and cannot walk easily. Because the horse has *gone lame*, it cannot pull the carriage.

75 **strawberries** (page 84)
soft, sweet, red fruit.

76 **expecting a child** – *to expect a child* (page 87)
going to have a baby. Pregnant.

77 **ma'am** (page 90)
a shortened form of *madam* – a polite way of talking to a woman in the nineteenth century.

78 **ashamed** – *to be ashamed* (page 91)
feel very bad because you, or someone who you know, has done something wrong.

79 **funeral** (page 94)
a ceremony that takes place after someone dies. After the *funeral*, the body of the dead person is buried in the ground, or it is burnt in a fire – it is cremated.

80 **attachment** (page 95)

a way of saying that a person has met someone who they like very much and they want to be with them.

81 **been true** – *to be true to someone* (page 96)

Jane loves Frank very much. She has not told anyone about their secret engagement. This was Frank's wish. She has *been true to him*.

82 **envy** – *to envy* (page 103)

having an unhappy feeling because you want to be like someone else, or have their things.

83 **mourning** (page 109)

a period of time when people live quietly and remember a person who has died. In Britain, people used to wear black clothes when they were *mourning*.

84 **performed their marriage ceremony** (page 113)

when a clergyman or vicar speaks special words at the marriage of a man and a woman, he is *performing a marriage ceremony*.

85 **poultry-house** (page 114)

a small building where chickens are kept. *Poultry* is the word used for a group of chickens. At the time of this story, most families kept animals such as chickens, pigs and cows near their houses. They ate the eggs from their own chickens, drank the milk from their own cows and ate the meat – the pork – from their own pigs.

Exercises

People In The Story

Put the names in the box next to the correct description.

> Frank Churchill   Mr Robert Martin   Harriet Smith
> ~~Mr Elton~~   John Knightley   Mr Henry Woodhouse
> Emma Woodhouse   Mr George Knightley   Jane Fairfax

1	The vicar of Highbury. He was young and not married at the start of the story.	*Mr Elton*
2	The owner of Donwell Abbey. He was the only man who could tell Emma she was wrong.	
3	The manager of a farm near Donwell Abbey.	
4	The owner of Hartfield House. He had two daughters and had been a widower for many years.	
5	The son of Mr Weston by his first marriage.	
6	She was the leader of polite society in the neighbourhood of Highbury. She was pretty, clever and rich.	
7	A clever lawyer who lived in London and often visited Donwell Abbey.	
8	A pupil at Mrs Goddard's school. She had beautiful blue eyes and fair hair, but she was not very clever.	
9	The orphaned daughter of an army lieutenant.	

Multiple Choice

Tick the best answer.

Q1   Who does Mr Knightley think is an unsuitable friend for Emma?
     a Frank Churchill.
     b Miss Biggs.
     c Mr Elton.
     d Harriet Smith. ✓

Q2   Why doesn't Emma want Harriet to marry Mr Roberts?
     a Because Emma is jealous.
     b Because she doesn't want her friend to marry a poor farmer.
     c Because Harriet is already engaged to Frank Churchill.
     d Because Emma wants Harriet to marry Mr Knightley.

Q3   What reason does Mr Knightley give for Emma's dislike of
     Jane Fairfax?
     a Emma is jealous of Jane's education.
     b Emma is jealous of Jane's money.
     c Emma is jealous of Jane's house.
     d Emma is jealous of Jane's clothes.

Q4   Who sends Jane Fairfax a piano as a present?
     a Mr Knightley.
     b Colonel Campbell.
     c Mr Dixon.
     d Frank Churchill.

Q5   Mr Woodhouse is initially unhappy about Emma's engagement.
     What makes him change his mind?
     a Mr Knightley suggests both Emma and her father move in
        with him.
     b Mr Woodhouse decides to marry Mrs Bates.
     c Mr Knightley suggests moving in with the Woodhouses.
     d Emma promises to visit him every day.

Words From The Story 1

Write each word from the box next to the correct meaning.

> suitable   funeral   inherit   neighbourhood   widower
> attachment   governess   flatter   ~~draught~~   spoil   quarrel   blame

1	cold air that comes into a room	*draught*
2	something which is joined to something else, also a feeling of love or friendship between people	
3	the time when a dead person is buried or cremated	
4	to say that someone has done something wrong	
5	to talk angrily with someone because you do not agree	
6	to go bad (of food), also to give children too much (money) and make them think they can have anything they want	
7	to try to please people by saying nice things about them – usually to gain their friendship or help	
8	a woman who lived and worked in the house of a rich family; her job was to look after the children and teach them	
9	a man whose wife is dead	
10	the local area, the houses and streets near the place where you live, synonym – vicinity	
11	right for somebody or something, synonym – appropriate	
12	to get money and property from the will of a dead person	

Words From The Story 2

Rewrite each of the sentences. Replace the underlined words using one from the story.

Example	*Emma did not think that Robert Martin was <u>good enough</u> for Harriet Smith.*
ANSWER	She did not think that Robert Martin was suitable for Harriet Smith.

1   Emma did not like Jane Fairfax because her manner was <u>cold and unfriendly</u>.
    Jane Fairfax's manner was

2   Mr Elton married a woman who had <u>been left a lot of money</u> by her dead husband.
    Mr Elton married a woman who had

3   Frank Churchill had to <u>make arrangement because his mother had died</u>.
    Frank Churchill had to arrange his mother's

4   Emma did not believe that Frank Churchill and Jane Fairfax were <u>engaged</u>.
    Emma did not believe that there was

5   When Harriet refused Robert Martin's proposal of marriage, George Knightley <u>said that it was Emma's fault</u>.
    George Knightley

6   Frank Churchill made arrangements for <u>a dancing party</u> at the local inn.
    Frank Churchill arranged

7   Old Mr Woodhouse had a great dislike of <u>cold air from open doors and windows</u>.
    Mr Woodhouse disliked

8   Mrs Elton knew several rich families who required <u>a teacher to work in their houses</u>.
    The families required

Words From The Story 3

Unjumble the letters to find words from the story. The meanings are given to help you.

Example	LURECHEF
MEANING	happy and good tempered
ANSWER	*cheerful*

1   SEROMIME
MEANING   events you remember
ANSWER

_____

2   NALMETENG
MEANING   an educated and polite man
ANSWER

_____

3   SUNDRAGIA
MEANING   people who look after a child whose parents are dead
ANSWER

_____

4   STEGUS
MEANING   people who are invited to a house or party
ANSWER

_____

5   TANTENTIO
MEANING   notice, interest
ANSWER

_____

6   TENMEGANGE
MEANING   an arrangement to be married
ANSWER

_____

7   ONIONIP
MEANING   what you think about something
ANSWER

_____

Making Sentences 1

Rearrange the words to make sentences.

Example	*life hated Mr Woodhouse in his changes*
ANSWER	Mr Woodhouse hated changes in his life.

1 the little family's cottage reached Harriet and poor Emma

_____

2 could The pretty farmer make a better than with the young match girl

_____

3 last time I had a very pleasant night

_____

4 Miss Someone has sent a piano Fairfax

_____

5 a wife has chosen very unsuitable Mr Elton

_____

6 the weather of the day was the ball and It was wet

_____

7 They a group of girls who met the gypsies asked for money

_____

8 The one marriage of a Mrs George and Mr Knightley was long and happy

_____

133

Making Sentences 2

Write questions for the answers.

Example	***What*** *does Emma call her father?*
ANSWER	Emma calls her father 'Papa.'

Q1   *Why*
A1   Emma told Harriet to refuse Robert Martin's proposal because he was unsuitable.

Q2   *How*
A2   Mr Weston had made money in trade.

Q3   *Where*
A3   The people in polite society's money came from inheritance.

Q4   *Who*
A4   Frank Churchill met Jane Fairfax in Weymouth.

Q5   *Why*
A5   No one knew that Jane and Frank were engaged because they did not tell anyone.

Q6   *When*
A6   Mr Elton went to Bath after proposing marriage to Emma.

Q7   *How long*
A7   Mr Elton stayed in Bath for only three weeks before getting married.

Q8   *What*
A8   Emma said that Mrs Elton was vulgar.

Q9   *Who*
A9   Emma thought that Frank wanted to marry her.

Q10   *How much*
A10   George Knightley was seventeen years older than Emma.

Grammar Focus

Write nouns for the verbs. Follow the pattern for each column.

Pattern 1		Pattern 2		Pattern 3	
VERB	NOUN	VERB	NOUN	VERB	NOUN
refuse	*refusal*	enclose	*enclosure*	oppose	*opposition*
propose		expose		expose	
dispose		disclose		propose	
remove		erase		suppose	

Note: both *propose* and *expose* are in two of the columns. The nouns have different meanings.

Story Focus

Complete the gaps with names from the box.

> George Knightley   Robert Martin   Anne Taylor   Jane Fairfax
> Mr Weston   Emma Woodhouse   Frank Churchill   Harriet Smith

_____ marries _____

_____ marries _____

_____ marries _____

_____ marries _____

Published by Macmillan Heinemann ELT
Between Towns Road, Oxford OX4 3PP
Macmillan Heinemann ELT is an imprint of
Macmillan Publishers Limited
Companies and representatives throughout the world
Heinemann is a registered trademark of Pearson Education, used under licence

ISBN 978 0 2300 3527 0
ISBN 978 1 4050 7454 4 (with CD pack)

This version of *Emma* by Jane Austen was retold by
Margaret Tarner for Macmillan Readers
First published 2005
Text © Macmillan Publishers Limited 2005
Design and illustration © Macmillan Publishers Limited 2005

This version first published 2005

Illustrated by Ruth Palmer
Cover by Getty Images\Bridgeman Art Archive

Printed in Thailand
2011 2010 2009
6 5 4 3 2

with CD pack
2011 2010 2009
11 10 9 8 7

V